THE GREEN LEAF BIBLE SERIES

Heroes of the Bible

Year One

"The whole Bible for the whole church"

Copyright © 1982 by Green Leaf Press

All rights reserved. No part of this book may be used or reproduced in any manner whatsoever without written permission, except in the case of brief quotations embodied in critical articles and reviews.

ISBN 0-938462-05-9 (set)
ISBN 0-938462-06-7 (Year One)

The scripture quotations in this publication are from the Revised Standard Version of the Bible copyrighted 1946, 1952 © 1971, 1973 by the Division of Christian Education of the National Council of the Churches of Christ in the U.S.A., and used by permission.

GREEN LEAF PRESS, P.O. BOX 6880, Alhambra, California   91802

PRINTED IN THE UNITED STATES OF AMERICA

THE GREEN LEAF BIBLE SERIES

Year One: Heroes of the Bible

Foster H. Shannon, Senior Editor

Lois M. Rew, Associate Editor

Grace Cox, Contributing Editor

Bette Johansen, Contributing Editor

CONTENTS

PREFACE	5
BASIC PRINCIPLES	7
RESOURCE MATERIAL	10
SCRIPTURE MEMORY PROGRAM	12
FIVE/SIX YEAR PLAN	14
UNIT ONE, GENESIS (13 WEEKS)	15
UNIT TWO, LUKE (17 WEEKS)	51
UNIT THREE, EXODUS (11 WEEKS)	101
UNIT FOUR, PAUL I (11 WEEKS)	139

PREFACE

The Green Leaf Bible Series is a truly new Sunday School and/or Bible study curriculum. It is comprehensive in its approach providing for the study of the whole Bible in a six-year period. It does not seek to do for the teacher what the teacher can do for himself. For example, there is no attempt to narrate for the teacher the passage to be studied. Such a process may short-circuit the study of the passage that the teacher should be engaged in--reading and digesting the material for himself so that he may relate it in the most meaningful context possible for his particular class.

This material has been developed over a period of over ten years in actual (not theoretical) teaching situations. We know that it works, and that it does not take an especially skilled Sunday School teacher to use it. Without engaging the teacher in a lot of superfluous reading, an abundance of material is provided so that the teacher can design the lesson that best fits his pupils and age range.

Since this material has been developed in the context of local churches, perhaps we should mention that it is not a denominational curriculum. It is a biblical curriculum. One half hour spent perusing this Year One Teacher's Manual should establish that fact to anyone's satisfaction. We very much believe this material to be in harmony, first of all with the Bible itself, and then with the mainstream of historic Christianity. The guiding principle throughout is of inductive not deductive Bible study. Christian doctrine must derive from the Bible and be continually tested by the Bible (see Acts 17:11).

The best way to use the Green Leaf Bible Series is to have the lesson taught and discussed by the pastor, associate pastor, or a senior teacher at a weekly meeting of all Sunday School teachers. An alternate to that plan is to have bi-weekly or even monthly meetings of the teaching staff where the major themes of the unit in consideration are presented and discussed. At such a meeting resource materials may be evaluated and teachers may discuss the best possibilities for lesson plans and use of resources appropriate for each department. In addition to the general resources suggested in this series -- it is most helpful if each church using this curriculum will prepare a resource list for each unit utilizing those pictures, maps, film strips, etc. that are currently on hand in the church and appropriate for that unit.

The Green Leaf Bible Series is a fresh approach because it is comprehensive, thoroughly biblical, geared to maximize the time that the teacher spends in Bible study, and with all that it is brief and simple so that the plan can be easily grasped. We believe that it provides one of the most effective instruments to assist the teacher with profitable Bible teaching at all age levels from Primary to Adult.

Immanuel Presbyterian Church have contributed to the final form of this curriculum.

Especially involved in assistance with this volume have been Associate Editor, Lois Rew, and Assistant Editors, Grace Cox and Bette Johansen. Manuscript typing and many details of oversight have been in the competent hands of Jo Apel. Anita Heihn has handled all the graphics work in a most able and gracious manner.

The theme of this curriculum is, "The whole Bible for the whole church." We believe that it will aid many churches to teach the Bible in an appealing and effective manner. We trust that it will be an instrument in the hands of the Holy Spirit to lead many to Christ, to more fully appreciate the counsels of God, and to delight to do the will and work of God.

Foster H. Shannon, Senior Editor
THE GREEN LEAF BIBLE SERIES

BASIC PRINCIPLES

Basic Assumptions and Guidelines

1. The Bible is the inspired word of God, true as a whole and in all of its parts. While it is not a manual of science, history, or geography, it does not contradict or deny truth at any point. The Bible uses paradox and seemingly opposing truths in dialectical tension to reveal God and his purposes, but it does not contradict itself in an ultimate sense. The main purpose of the Bible is to instruct people how they may have a vital, living, eternal relationship with God.

2. Sunday School and other Bible teachers should spend their best time studying the biblical text rather than expansive and sometimes tedious manuals about the Sunday School lesson.

3. Projects are not identified according to appropriate age range, because the individual teacher should be the best judge of which projects are suitable to his or her class.

4. The quiz at the end of each study section serves at least two purposes:
   a) it puts a quiz in the teacher's hands that can be given to each pupil
   b) it suggests minimum learning goals for each section. For this purpose, the teacher should refer to the quiz at the beginning of the study and from time to time during the period of study.

   The biblical material must not only be covered in class, it must be learned! The quizzes provide a means of stimulating and evaluating the learning process.

   The quiz may be used in a number of ways:
   a) it can be given to students as is
   b) it can be modified by the teacher and then given to the students
   c) it can form the basis for a contest between two teams on the final week of the study
   d) it can be used as a basis for discussion in order to review the study material

5. The entire Bible is covered in a series of twenty-four units over a period of six years. Most of the material may be covered in a five-year cycle by making certain substitutions. There are four study units per year. The series is comprised of six teacher's manuals, one for each year, plus supplementary workbooks and other supplementary materials that may be added at the discretion of the organization ordering the materials.

The following principles have been followed in developing this series of studies:
- a) units are alternated between the Old Testament and New Testament
- b) one of the gospels is to be studied each year in the general period involving Christmas and Easter
- c) a general chronological approach to historical sections
- d) the life and writings of the Apostle Paul are divided into five sections; one section per year for the first five years
- e) frequent review to strengthen understanding
- f) memory verses are keyed to the curriculum and made an integral part of the program

Teacher Preparation

Most of the weekly lessons have *more* material than can be adequately utilized in the relatively brief Sunday School period. If possible, the teacher should at least lightly touch on each subject in the scripture to be covered. Going over the accompanying outline, of the book of the Bible under study, could be helpful at this point. On the other hand, the teacher should feel neither obligation or compulsion to deal in detail with every possible theme. Each teacher (or Sunday School department personnel) should decide the emphasis to give within each lesson.

This is much more material than can be adequately dealt with in the space of an hour. The teacher will need to decide what sections will get only slight treatment--those that will get somewhat more attention--and possibly the one or two sections that will get top priority.

Ordinarily a teacher will especially prepare for one or two sections within the lesson and will not prepare equally for all sections. Of course, the age range and needs of the class will be substantial factors in choosing the material to be emphasized.

Weekly Lesson Plan

1. Pray for God's help and guidance. Pray for each pupil at least once a week.

2. Read the passage, being ready to underline significant verses or make notes in a notebook.

3. Read over the lesson. Make notes on the lesson sheet. Indicate ideas you want to especially emphasize. List additional things that you want to do.

4. It is helpful to prepare an outline or lesson plan for each class period. What follows is a suggestion--the details will vary from program to program:

Opening Prayer

Roll - Greetings - Introduction of visitors

Special Activities/Offering

Introduction of and/or review of memory verses

Review of last week's lesson and assignments

Tell the current lesson in your own words and/or have students read all or part of passage

Use illustrative and/or other support materials

Assign and/or work on projects

Discuss passage--seeking to draw out Basic Concepts and keeping overall goals in mind

Closing sharing and prayer time

5. Be in your classroom ahead of schedule to make sure everything is in readiness for your class.

GENERAL RESOURCE MATERIAL

BOOKS

The Bible Almanac, J. I. Packer, M.C. Tenney, W. White, Jr., Eds.
  Thomas Nelson
Compact Bible Atlas (Revised Edition), Charles F. Pfeiffer, Baker Book House
Cruden's Concordance, Alexander Cruden, Baker Book House
Everyday Life in Bible Times, National Geographic Society
  (The text is sometimes disappointing to those with a high view of the
  inspiration of scripture. But the illustrations are excellent, and overall
  it is worthwhile.)
Historical Atlas to the Bible, Westminster Press
Hurlbut's Story of the Bible, Zondervan
Jerusalem in the Time of Jesus, Joachim Jeremias, Fortress Press (paper)
The New Bible Commentary, Inter-Varsity
The New Bible Dictionary, Inter-Varsity
Pictorial Bible Atlas, E. Blaiklock, Ed., Zondervan
A Picture Dictionary of the Bible, Abingdon Press

MAPS, CHARTS, TIMELINES

Maps of Bible Lands (8 maps, 42" X 31" with folding tripod), Abingdon
Bible Maps and Charts (11 Old Testament, 9 New Testament, 2 Bible Through
  the Centuries), David C. Cook
Bible Maps and Charts, Standard Publishing Co.
Bible Time Line (wall chart, characters and events), Standard Publishing Co.
Chronological and Background Charts of the Old Testament, H. Wayne House,
  Zondervan
Class Maps (22" X 28" with tripod), Cokesbury
The Lands of the Bible Today, National Geographic Society
Press and Make Bible Maps, Abingdon Press

ACTIVITY BOOKS, PROJECTS, GAMES, PUZZLES

New Bible Squares: Meeting Bible People (age 7 to adult), Standard Publishing
  Co.
Bible Card Games: Authors, Battles, Daughters, Charades, Who Am I (grades
  1 and 2), What Am I, Zondervan
Bible Treasure Hunt (age 10 to adult), Standard Publishing Co.

Resource Suppliers

Abingdon Press, 201 Eighth Ave., S., Nashville, TN 37203
Accent Publications, P.O. Box 15337, Denver, CO 80215
American Bible Society, P.O. Box 5656, Grand Central Station, New York,
  NY 10163
Augsberg Publishing House, 426 S. Fifth St., Minneapolis, MN 55415
Baptist Sunday School Board, 127 Ninth Ave. North, Nashville, TN 37234

Cokesbury (Regional Service Centers)
  1661 N. Northwest Hwy., Park Ridge, IL 60068
  1600 Queen Anne Rd., Teaneck, NJ 07666
  5th and Grace, P.O. Box 298, Richmond, VA 23261
  201 Eighth Ave., S., Nashville, TN 37202
  1910 Main St., P.O. Box 298, Dallas, TX 75221
  1635 Adrian Rd., Burlingame, CA 94010
Concordia Publishing Co., 3558 S. Jefferson Ave., St. Louis, MO 63118
Eerdmans Publishing Co. 255 Jefferson Ave., S.E., Grand Rapids, MI 49503
Ideals Publishing Co., 11315 Watertown Plank Rd., Milwaukee, WI 53226
International Child Evangelism Fellowship, Inc., 800 N. Clark St.,
  Chicago, IL 60610
Inter-Varsity Press, 5206 Main St., Downers Grove, IL 60515
Moody Press, 820 N. LaSalle St., Chicago, IL 60610
Thomas Nelson, Inc., P.O. Box 946, Nashville, TN 37203
Presbyterian Publishing House, 341 Ponce de Leon Ave., N.E.
  Atlanta, Georgia 30365
Scripture Press Publications, Inc., 1825 College Ave., Wheaton, IL 60187
Standard Publishing Co., 8121 Hamilton Ave., Cincinnatti, OH 45231
Warner Press, Box 2499, Anderson, IN 46011
The Westminster Press, 925 Chestnut St. Philadelphia, PA 19107
Word, Inc., Box 1790, Waco, TX 76703
Zondervan Publishing Co., 1415 Lake Dr., S.E., Grand Rapids,
  MI 49506

Perodicals

The National Geographic is a rich source of background material for Bible study. Make a list of those issues that have helpful articles and see if people will donate them for reference use in your Christian Education program.

We do not endorse the content of all the articles in Biblical Archaeology Review. Nonetheless; it is an almost indispensable resource for Sunday School and Bible study programs. A subscription would be useful to most churches: Biblical Archaeology Review, 3000 Connecticut Ave., NW, #300, Washington, DC 20008.

SCRIPTURE MEMORY PROGRAM

One of the principles of the Green Leaf Bible Series is that the memorization of key passages of scripture should be an integral part of a Sunday School/Bible Study program. The memorization of scripture serves several purposes: It facilitates the individual's personal relationship with Jesus Christ in that wherever a person is, whatever the circumstances, whatever the time of day or night there are passages of scripture available that can be thought about--considered--meditated upon. Christians are frequently hamstrung in sharing their faith with others by their inability either to recall or to find in the Bible specific passages of scripture. The memorization of scripture will enhance one's personal relationship with the Lord. It provides a foundation for effective witness. And it also significantly assists in developing a framework for understanding the major themes and doctrines of the Bible.

All of these passages of scripture are related to the study program on a month-by-month basis. And most of them are closely related to the passage of scripture being studied for that particular month.

Some passages of scripture that themselves emphasize or encourage the memorization of scripture are as follows:

Deuteronomy 6:6, "And these words which I command you this day shall be upon your heart;"

Deuteronomy 11:18, "You shall therefore lay up these words of mine in your heart and in your soul; and you shall bind them as a sign upon your hand, and they shall be as frontlets between your eyes."

Psalm 119:11, "I have laid up thy word in my heart, that I might not sin against thee."

Proverbs 7:2,3, "keep my commandments and live, keep my teachings as the apple of your eye; bind them on your fingers, write them on the tablet of your heart."

I Peter 3:15, "Always be prepared to make a defense to anyone who calls you to account for the hope that is in you,..."

Matthew 4:1-11: Note Jesus' use of scripture that was written on his heart in rejecting the temptations of the devil.

The seventy-two verses listed by year appear below:

Year One
Genesis 1:27
Romans 3:23
II Timothy 2:15
Luke 9:23
Luke 2:52
John 16:24
James 3:17
Titus 3:5
Romans 10:9,10
Galatians 6:7,8
Colossians 3:1,2
Colossians 3:17

Year Two
Deuteronomy 6:4,5
Joshua 1:8
I Peter 3:15
Matthew 7:12
John 13:34,35
John 14:1-3
John 15:5
Acts 16:31
Acts 17:11
Ephesians 6:10,11
Romans 12:2
II Timothy 1:7

Year Three
Acts 1:8
Acts 4:12
Acts 2:42
Matthew 6:33
Matthew 21:22
Matthew 4:19
Matthew 28:19,20
Psalm 23:1-3
Psalm 23:4-6
Ephesians 2:8,9
Philippians 4:4
Philippians 4:8

Year Four
Proverbs 3:5,6
Ecclesiastes 12:1
Proverbs 16:3
I Corinthians 13:4-7
John 3:16,17
John 1:12
John 5:24
John 8:31b,32
Romans 5:1
Romans 5:8
Romans 8:1
Proverbs 11:24

Year Five
Hebrews 10:25
Hebrews 11:6
Hebrews 4:12
II Corinthians 3:18
II Corinthians 5:17
I Corinthians 10:13
I Corinthians 15:58
Ezra 7:10
Malachi 3:10
Revelation 3:20
I John 1:9
James 1:5

Year Six
Isaiah 1:18
Micah 6:8
Hosea 10:12
Philippians 1:6
Galatians 5:22,23
II Timothy 2:2
II Timothy 3:16,17
Psalm 1:1-3
Psalm 1:4-6
Psalm 119:11
Jeremiah 33:3
Proverbs 21:31

THE GREEN LEAF BIBLE SERIES

Five/Six Year Plan

	←— 13 weeks —→	←——— 17 weeks ———→	←— 11 weeks —→	←— 11 weeks —→
	Sep　Oct　Nov	Dec　Jan　Feb　Mar	Apr　May　Jun	Jun　Jul　Aug
Year One	Genesis (13)	Luke (17)	Exodus (11)	Paul I (11)
Year Two	Sinai to Samuel (13) (includes Ruth)	The Period Between the Testaments (4) Mark (13)	Paul II (11)	Samuel and Saul (11)
Year Three	Peter (9) James and Jude (4)	Matthew (17)	David (11)	Paul III (11)
Year Four	Solomon (13)	John (17)	Paul IV-Romans (5) Job (6) or Minor Prophets	Division of Kingdom (11)
Year Five	Hebrews (8) Exile (5) (Daniel and Esther)	Paul V, Corinthians (8) Pre-Reformation History (4) Post-Reformation History (5) or Correlation of Gospels: The Life of Christ (17)	Return (5) (Ezra, Haggai, Zechariah Nehemiah, Malachi) Jonah and Nahum (3) Ezekiel (3) or Isaiah (6)	Second Coming (6) Letters of John (5) or Psalms (11)
Year Six	Isaiah (6) Minor Prophets (7) (Obadiah, Hosea, Joel, Amos, Micah, Habakkuk, Zephaniah)	Correlation of Gospels: The Life of Christ (17)	Psalms (11)	Jeremiah and Lamentations (5) Review of Bible History (6)

Genesis

THE BOOK OF GENESIS

CURRICULUM RESOURCE LIST   APPROXIMATE PRICE

BOOKS

My Book of Bible Stories; Standard	6.95
Arch Books; Concordia	.79
"A Garden and a Promise"	
"The Story of Noah's Ark"	
"The Boy Who Saved His Family" (Joseph)	
Bible Story Cartoons, Norman Lynch; Standard	
The Old Testament in 16 books (in case)	9.95
Book 1: "Creation, Adam and Eve, Noah and the Ark"	.59
Book 2: "Tower of Babel, Abraham, Isaac"	.59
Book 3: "Isaac's Wells, Perils of Jacob"	.59
Book 4: "Joseph and His Brothers"	.59
If You Lived in Bible Times; Victor Books: Scripture Press	6.95

MAPS, CHARTS, TIMELINES

Chronological and Background Charts of the Old Testament; Zondervan	10.95

TRANSPARENCIES, DUPLICATING MASTERS, FILMSTRIPS, FILMS

Filmstrips: Concordia Audio Visual Media		5.75
"Jacob, Bearer of the Promise"		
"Joseph, The Young Man"		
"Joseph, The Ruler of Egypt"		
"Abraham, Man of Faith"		
Record to go with above filmstrips		3.45
Complete set of four filmstrips and records		32.75
Storyline Films; American Bible Society	Purchase	40.00
	Rental	7.50
"How the World Began"		
"Two and Two" (Noah)		
"Rainbow Promise" (Noah)		
Jensen Bible Study Charts (Transparencies); Moody		9.95
General Survey: Volume I		
Old Testament: Volume II		
Old Testament Puzzles Masters; Standard		5.95

FLANNELGRAPH, POSTERS, PICTURES

Creation; International Child Evangelism Fellowship	6.49
Noah and the Ark; Scripture Press	3.50
Joseph; International Child Evangelism Fellowship	6.49
Joseph the Dreamer; Scripture Press	3.50
Joseph in Egypt; Scripture Press	3.50

GREEN LEAF BIBLE SERIES

YEAR ONE, UNIT ONE

THE BOOK OF GENESIS

Week One	THE CREATION OF ALL THINGS	Genesis 1:1-2:3
Week Two	ADAM AND EVE	Genesis 2:4-5:32
Week Three	NOAH	Genesis 6:1-9:29
Week Four	THE TOWER OF BABEL	Genesis 10:1-11:32
Week Five	THE CALL AND RESPONSE OF ABRAHAM	Genesis 12:1-14:24
Week Six	THE PROMISE OF A SON TO ABRAHAM	Genesis 15:1-18:33
Week Seven	THE SAVING OF LOT	Genesis 19:1-21:34
Week Eight	THE GREAT TEST OF ABRAHAM	Genesis 22:1-25:18
Week Nine	ISAAC AND JACOB	Genesis 25:19-27:45
Week Ten	JACOB IN THE HOUSEHOLD OF LABAN	Genesis 27:46-30:43
Week Eleven	JACOB'S RETURN TO CANAAN	Genesis 31:1-36:43
Week Twelve	THE STORY OF JOSEPH	Genesis 37:1-50:26
Week Thirteen	REVIEW AND QUIZ	

Genesis

INTRODUCTION: THE BOOK OF GENESIS

The authorship of Genesis has traditionally been accorded to Moses. However, Mosaic authorship has been questioned in some quarters in the past one hundred years. The first five books of the Bible (the Pentateuch) are said by some to be the product of later Israel (800-600 B.C.). Jesus and the Apostles referred to the books of Moses (Matthew 19:7,8; Mark 10:3; Luke 16:29-31; Luke 24:27; Acts 3:22; Mark 12:26; II Corinthians 3:15). The solidly established tradition of the Mosaic authorship of the first five books of the Bible is surely rooted in the fact that Moses was the author of these books.

Moses' education and training in Egypt, the fact that he was the spiritual and temporal leader of the Israelites, and the forty years in the Sinai wilderness--all indicate the necessary background and time for Moses to be the author. This would mean that these books were written about 1400 B.C. Many of the events in Genesis took place long before Moses' lifetime. Moses must have depended upon both oral and written tradition. The narrative relies in part on direct revelation by God to Moses. We see such direct revelation in the call of Moses, the Ten Commandments, and the moral and ritual law which are recorded in the other books of the Pentateuch.

All people, Christians and non-Christians alike, need some humility about the limitation of their knowledge when they come to a study of the book of Genesis. "The book describes the beginning of the universe, the beginning of man, the beginning of human sin, the beginning of salvation, the beginning of the Hebrew people, as well as the beginning of many other things." (New Bible Commentary, page 75). The Genesis account of creation does not exactly conform to modern concepts of the development of the universe. However, it is more in accord with modern than with ancient concepts, which points to its Divine origin.

The main characters of the book are Adam, Noah, Abraham, Isaac, Jacob, and Joseph. Adam was the first man, and in him all men sinned. Genesis depicts God's creation and man's corruption of that creation through sin. In Genesis the foundation for God's redemption of his creation is laid. It begins with judgment, but it includes hope. God reestablishes his relationship with man through Seth. Of the three sons of Noah: Ham, Shem, and Japeth, God especially works through the line of Shem.

God establishes a covenant relationship with Abraham, one of the decendants of Shem. God calls Abraham, establishes a covenant with him, and blesses him. God promises not only to bless Abraham, but to make him a blessing to all the peoples of the world (Genesis 12:3; 15:5; 17:5; 22:18). The New Testament tells us that this promise is ultimately fulfilled in Jesus Christ and the church (Romans 4:16,17; Galatians 3:6-9;

GREEN LEAF BIBLE SERIES

Romans 2:28,29; 4:11,12). It is to Abraham and his descendants that God continues his self-revelation. It is through the nation of Israel that mankind learns more definitely about God and how he is to be worshiped. And it is through the line of Abraham: Adam-Seth-Noah-Shem-Abraham-Isaac-Jacob-Judah-David that Jesus Christ, the Messiah, the Savior of the world, is born.

OUTLINE OF GENESIS

  I. BEGINNINGS (1-11)
      1. Creation (1)
      2. Adam and Eve (2,3)
      3. Abel and Cain (4)
      4. Genealogy (5) Antediluvian ancestors
      5. Noah (6-9)
      6. Table of Nations (10)
      7. Tower of Babel (11:1-9)
      8. The line of descent from Shem to Abraham (11:10-32)

  II. ABRAHAM (12:1-25:18)
      1. The call and response of Abraham (12:1-9)
      2. Abraham journeys to Egypt (12:10-19)
      3. Abraham and Lot agree to occupy separate territories (13)
      4. The Battle of the Sheiks--Abraham rescues Lot (14)
      5. Abraham promised a son of his own and a great inheritance (15)
      6. Sarah and Abraham seek a son through Hagar (26)
      7. God renews his covenant with Abraham--males to be circumcised (17)
      8. Abraham's conversation with the three angels (18)
      9. Lot rescued from Sodom and Gomorrah (19)
      10. Abraham and Abimelech (20)

Genesis

11. Isaac is born (21)

12. Abraham commanded to present Isaac as a sacrifice (22)

13. The death of Sarah--arrangements for her burial (23)

14. Isaac bethrothed to Rebekah (24)

15. The death and burial of Abraham (25:1-18)

III. JACOB (25:19-36:43)
    1. Jacob and his parents (25:19-27:45)
       a. The birth of Jacob and Esau (25:19-28)
       b. Jacob purchases Esau's birthright with bread and pottage (29:29-34)
       c. The Lord renews the covenant with Isaac (26:1-5)
       d. Isaac's dealings with the Philistines (26:6-23)
       e. Jacob deprives Esau of his Father's blessing by deceit (26:34-27:45)

    2. Jacob's Journey to Paddan-aram (27:46-28:22)
       a. He is sent forth by Isaac and Rebekah (27:46-28:22)
       b. Esau takes a wife of the Ishmaelites in addition to his Canaanite wives (28:6-9)
       c. Jacob's dream (28:20-22)

    3. Jacob in the household of Laban (29:1-30:43)
       a. Jacob is married to Rachel and Leah (29:1-30:43)
       b. The offspring of Jacob (29:31-30:24)
       c. Laban and Jacob agree regarding the assignment of the flocks (30:25-43)

    4. Jacob's return to Canaan (31:1-36:43)
       a. God directs Jacob to return to Canaan (31:1-55)
       b. Jacob's encounter with Esau (32:1-33:20)
       c. Jacob's sons slaughter and plunder a city (34:1-31)
       d. Jacob moves to Bethel (35:1-29)
       e. The descendants of Esau (36:1-43)

IV. JOSEPH (37:1-50:26)
    1. Joseph as a youth (37:1-36)
       a. Joseph's dream (37:1-11)
       b. Joseph sold into slavery by his brothers (37:12-28)
       c. Jacob mourns for Joseph (37:29-36)

    2. Judah and Tamar (38:1-30)

    3. Joseph as a slave (39:1-41:36)

GREEN LEAF BIBLE SERIES

      a. Joseph in Potiphar's household (39:1-18)
      b. Joseph in prison (39:19-40:23)
      c. Joseph interprets Pharoah's dream (41:1-36)

4. Joseph as a great leader of government (41:37-45:28)
      a. Joseph appointed a ruler in Egypt (41:37-57)
      b. Jacob sends ten sons to Egypt to buy grain (42:1-38)
      c. Jacob sends his sons a second time (43:1-44:34)
      d. Jacob makes himself known to his brothers (45:1-28)

5. Israel comes to Egypt (46:1-47:12)
      a. Jacob comes to Egypt (46:1-27)
      b. Jacob and his family settled in the land of Goshen (46:28-47:12)

6. On behalf of the state, Joseph acquires all of the Egyptians' possessions in exchange for grain (47:13-26)

7. Conclusion (47:27-50:26)
      a. Jacob blesses Ephraim and Manasseh (47:27-48:22)
      b. Jacob's prophecy and blessing upon his sons (49:1-27)
      c. The death and burial of Jacob (49:28-50:14)
      d. The death of Joseph (50:15-26)

Genesis

A List of the Abrahamic Covenant Affirmations of the Book of Genesis

12:1-3 (Abraham)
+ great nation
+ to be blessed by God
+ his name to be great
+ all the families of the earth to be blessed

12:7 (Abraham)
+ the land of Canaan promised to his descendants

13:14-17 (Abraham)
+ the land promised to Abraham and his descendants forever
+ his descendants to be exceedingly numerous

15:1-5 (Abraham)
+ a great reward promised
+ his own son
+ his descendants to be as numerous as the stars of heaven

15:13-16 (Abraham)
+ his descendants to be slaves in another land for 400 years
+ God will bring judgment on the nation that they serve and they will return to the land of Canaan

15:18-21 (Abraham)
+ a great extent of land promised

17:1-22 (Abraham)
+ to be the father of a multitude of nations
+ Abram/Abraham
+ an everlasting covenant
+ all the land of Canaan to be an everlasting possession
+ God will be the God of his descendants
+ circumcision as a sign of the covenant
+ Sarai/Sarah
  - to have a son/Isaac
  - a mother of nations
  - kings of peoples shall come from her
+ Ishmael to be the father of twelve and to become a great nation

22:15-18 (Abraham)
+ God will bless Abraham
+ his descendants to be exceedingly numerous and to possess the gates of their enemies
+ through his descendants all the nations of the earth to be blessed

26:23,24 (Isaac) (Beersheba)
+ God promises to bless Isaac and multiply his descendants

GREEN LEAF BIBLE SERIES

28:13-15 (Jacob) (Bethel)
+ the land
+ his descendants to be exceedingly numerous and to spread to the west, the east, the north, the south
+ by him and his descendants all the families of the earth are to be blessed

35:9-12 (Jacob)
+ new name: Israel
+ a company of nations and kings to come from him
+ promise of the land reaffirmed

46:2-4 (Jacob) (Beersheba)
+ Israel to be made a great nation in Egypt
+ God would go with them to Egypt and also would bring them out again

Addendum
1. There were a number of other occasions when God revealed himself in the book of Genesis, but the above are all of the occasions that related specifically to the covenant with Abraham, Isaac, and Jacob.

2. Note Joseph's awareness of an affirmation of that covenant: Genesis 50:24,25, "And Joseph said to his brothers, I am about to die; but God will visit you, and bring you up out of this land which he swore to Abraham, to Isaac, and to Jacob."

Genesis

Teacher's Outline

THE BOOK OF GENESIS

LESSON #1, THE CREATION OF ALL THINGS

PASSAGE TO STUDY: Genesis 1:1-2:3

SUGGESTIONS FOR SCRIPTURE TO BE READ IN CLASS
<table>
<tr><td>Basic</td><td>Supplementary</td></tr>
<tr><td>Genesis 1:1-5</td><td>Psalms 8, 19, 103, 104</td></tr>
<tr><td>Genesis 1:26</td><td>Romans 8:18-22</td></tr>
<tr><td></td><td>John 1:1</td></tr>
<tr><td></td><td>Colossians 1:15-20</td></tr>
<tr><td></td><td>Hebrews 1:2<u>6</u></td></tr>
</table>

SCRIPTURE MEMORY FOR SEPTEMBER (or for first month)
Genesis 1:27, "So God created man in his own image, in the image of God he created him; male and female he created them."

BASIC CONCEPTS
1. God is the source of all that is and, therefore, is all powerful and sovereign.

2. All people are created in the image of God (1:26, 27).

3. God has given human beings dominion over the creation (1:28-30).

4. The completeness/goodness of the creation.

5. The principle of a seventh day of rest (2:3).

GOALS
1. To better understand God's power and authority

2. To better understand God's good purpose in creation

3. To better understand man's proper relationship to God

4. To better understand man's proper relationship to the creation

5. To recommit ourselves to the principle of a day of rest

GREEN LEAF BIBLE SERIES

DISCUSSION QUESTIONS
1. What does the scripture mean that says, "So God blessed the seventh day and hallowed it," (Genesis 2:3)?

2. What rights and responsibilities has God given to man in relationship to the rest of the creation?

3. What are some of the implications of man being created in the image of God?

4. How do you understand the days of creation?

PROJECTS
1. Have microscope in class to view microscopic life.

2. Set up a display of beautiful pictures of mountains, rivers, plant life, animal life.

3. Display information and pictures of the galaxies which illustrate the scope of the universe.

4. Display pictures illustrating man's proper <u>dominion</u> of the earth.

5. Have each student prepare a list of the ways that man exercises dominion over the creation.

6. Discuss the proper uses of a day of rest.

7. Prepare portions of this scripture as a choral reading or litany.

8. Obtain public school science textbooks for a comparison of the treatment of creation.

9. Have students prepare a small book with pictures and stories of the seven days of creation.

Genesis

Teacher's Outline

THE BOOK OF GENESIS

LESSON #2, ADAM AND EVE

PASSAGE TO STUDY: Genesis 2:4-5:32

SUGGESTIONS FOR SCRIPTURE TO BE READ IN CLASS
<table>
<tr><td>Basic</td><td>Supplementary</td></tr>
<tr><td>Genesis 2:4-9</td><td>Romans 5:12-21</td></tr>
<tr><td>Genesis 2:15-25</td><td>I Corinthians 15:45-50</td></tr>
<tr><td>Genesis 3:1-7</td><td>Hebrews 11:4</td></tr>
<tr><td>Genesis 4:1-16</td><td>I John 3:11-18</td></tr>
</table>

SCRIPTURE MEMORY FOR SEPTEMBER
   Genesis 1:27, "So God created man in his own image, in the image of God he created him; male and female he created them."

BASIC CONCEPTS
   1. At the beginning man had a close relationship with God
       a. Genesis 1:27,28
       b. Genesis 2:7,8
       c. Genesis 2:15
       d. Genesis 3:8
       e. Genesis 3:21

   2. God made exceedingly generous provisions for mankind. See Genesis 1:28-30 and 2:15-25.

   3. The consequences of disbelief and disobedience are of the utmost seriousness
       a. Genesis 3:8-19
       b. Genesis 3:22-24
       c. Genesis 4:1-16

   4. The human marriage relationship is accorded great importance and significance. See Genesis 2:18-24.

GOALS
   1. To begin to understand the relationship that God intends to have with people

   2. To comprehend the nature of sin--the reason for man's broken

GREEN LEAF BIBLE SERIES

    relationship with God--and, therefore, the importance of salvation.

DISCUSSION QUESTIONS
1. What led to the disobedience of Adam and Eve?

2. Had God been fair to Adam and Eve?

3. What principles for marriage do we learn from this passage?

4. What was wrong with Cain's relationship with God?

PROJECTS
1. Have each student list some of the consequences of man's disobedience to God (sin). Then discuss the significance of the items on the list.

2. Have children draw scroll theater pictures with appropriate paraphrases of scripture to illustrate numbers 1 and 2 of basic concepts above.

3. Paste magazine pictures on a mural to illustrate "I am my brother's keeper."

4. List the steps in the temptation story of Genesis 3. Discuss how these steps could describe a situation that could happen in the children's lives.

5. Have students think about what there might be in their lives that might make them want to hide from God. Write a prayer in which they ask God's forgiveness for wrongdoing or thinking.

6. Read Genesis 3 aloud as a play using a narrator along with the various speaking parts.

Genesis

Teacher's Outline

THE BOOK OF GENESIS

LESSON #3, NOAH

PASSAGE TO STUDY: Genesis 6:1-9:29

SUGGESTIONS FOR SCRIPTURE TO BE READ IN CLASS

Basic	Supplementary
Genesis 6:11-22	Hebrews 11:7
Genesis 7:6-16	Psalms 103, 104:19-23
Genesis 7:27-8:5	Romans 1:18-32
Genesis 9:9-17	Matthew 24:37,38; Luke 17:26,27
	I Peter 3:18-22; 4:6
	II Peter 2:4-10

SCRIPTURE MEMORY FOR SEPTEMBER
Genesis 1:27, "So God created man in his own image, in the image of God he created him; male and female he created them."

BASIC CONCEPTS
1. The drastic contrast between life as God intends it and what people make of it

2. The fearful consequences of disobedience to God

3. The grace of God: the divine intention of save mankind

4. The ark as a symbol of Jesus Christ

5. God's covenant with the human race: "never again shall there be a flood to destroy the earth."

GOALS
1. To increase in comprehension of the holiness of God and, therefore, the fearful consequences of sin

2. To understand that God has an ultimate concern for his creation

3. To begin to understand the grace of God: that it is God's purpose to save all who will trust in him

4. To understand that God chose appropriate ways to carry out his program of salvation; for example, the choice of a particular family

GREEN LEAF BIBLE SERIES

5. To discuss God's purposes in establishing covenants with people emphasizing that the covenant is based upon God's character--not upon man's worth.

DISCUSSION QUESTIONS
1. Why did the people of Noah's day not heed God?

2. Some may think that the flood was a very severe judgment. What alternatives did God have, given the condition of the human race (Genesis 6:1-7)?

3. Why do people do things that hurt themselves?

4. Why does God go to the trouble of saving people?

PROJECTS
1. Have the class (or an individual) build a _simple_ model of the ark based on Genesis 6:14-16.

2. Discuss reasons for the flood. List alternatives to the flood.

3. List the evidences of the grace of God (disposition to forgive and heal) in this passage.

4. Draw pictures of the rainbow using such media as watercolor, wet chalk, crayon resist, etc. Use Genesis 8:22 or 9:13 as the picture caption.

5. Have a bulletin board display or ice cream carton decoupage to illustrate Genesis 8:22.

6. Discuss the ways in which God provided for Noah and the ways in which he provides for the child's family today.

7. Rainbow shrink art.

Genesis

Teacher's Outline

THE BOOK OF GENESIS

LESSON #4, THE TOWER OF BABEL

PASSAGE TO STUDY: Genesis 10:1-11:32

SUGGESTIONS FOR SCRIPTURE TO BE READ IN CLASS

Basic	Supplementary
Genesis 11:1-9	Acts 2:1-13 (Pentecost)
Psalm 103	Galatians 3:27,28
Matthew 1:1-17	
Luke 3:23-38	

SCRIPTURE MEMORY FOR SEPTEMBER
Genesis 1:27, "So God created man in his own image, in the image of God he created him; male and female he created them."

BASIC CONCEPTS
1. All of the people of the earth developed from the sons of Noah.

2. People have a strong and persistent inclination to live without God.

3. God sets limits to man's secularizing tendencies.

4. God continued his purpose of salvation through a particular family.

5. Progressive Revelation: Knowledge of God has increased progressively as God has dealt with people. The people that we read about in the book of Genesis did not have as much information about God as those in later times. We who have the whole Bible available to us, have more information about God and his purposes than those who had only a part of the Bible (see Hebrews 1:1).

GOALS
1. To emphasize our utter dependence upon God for knowledge about him, for sensitivity to that knowledge, and for the will to act upon it

2. To understand God's constancy: that he does not swerve from his purpose of salvation

GREEN LEAF BIBLE SERIES

DISCUSSION QUESTIONS
1. Why is so much information given to us regarding the descendants of Noah?

2. What was wrong with the attitude and activity of those who built the tower?

3. Why did God confuse the languages of various peoples or nations?

PROJECTS
1. Develop a genealogical chart showing the line of faith from Noah to Abram or develop a family tree with the same purpose.

2. Utilizing Genesis, chapter ten, and a Bible atlas or other reference material prepare a map indicating the major areas where the descendants of Noah were probably distributed.

3. List some of the ways that God reminds us of himself so that we do not forget about him; use information from the previous three lessons also.

Genesis

Teacher's Outline

THE BOOK OF GENESIS

LESSON #5, THE CALL AND RESPONSE OF ABRAHAM

PASSAGE TO STUDY: Genesis 12:1-14:24

SUGGESTIONS FOR SCRIPTURE TO BE READ IN CLASS

Basic	Supplementary
Genesis 12:1-9	Romans 4:1-25
Genesis 13:2-18	Galatians 3:6-29
	Acts 7:1-8
	Hebrews 7:1-10
	Hebrews 11:8-12; 17,18

SCRIPTURE MEMORY FOR OCTOBER:
   Romans 3:23, "since all have sinned and fall short of the glory of God,..."

BASIC CONCEPTS
1. Faith: what it means to take God at his word

2. Salvation: God's purpose in choosing Abraham to bring a blessing to all the families of the earth
   a. Genesis 12:1-3
   b. Genesis 13:14-16

3. Worship and Response to God: Abraham responded to the initiative of God by worshiping God and building altars which served as reminders of God's promises and provisions
   a. Genesis 12:7
   b. Genesis 12:8
   c. Genesis 13:3,4
   d. Genesis 13:18
   e. Genesis 14:18-20

4. Geography: the location of Ur of the Chaldeans, Haran, Canaan, Egypt, Bethel, the Salt Sea, Sodom and Gomorrah

5. The book of Genesis indicates a strong apologetic purpose in establishing property rights of the descendants of Abraham to the land of Canaan
   a. Genesis 12:1
   b. Genesis 12:7
   c. Genesis 13:14-17

GREEN LEAF BIBLE SERIES

    d. Genesis 15:7
    e. Genesis 15:18-20
    f. Genesis 23:3-20
    g. Genesis 25:9,10
    h. Genesis 26:1-4
    i. Genesis 28:13
    j. Genesis 35:12
       and other passages

GOALS
1. To be able to explain _faith_ in relation to something that God is asking the student to _do_

2. To be able to discuss the importance of worship and response to God

3. To be able to identify, on a map Ur of the Chaldeans, Haran, Canaan, Egypt, Bethel, the Salt Sea, Sodom and Gomorrah

DISCUSSION QUESTIONS
1. Recognizing the principle of _progressive revelation_, what were the essential elements to Abraham's knowledge of God?

2. How do we confirm our response when God speaks to us?

PROJECTS
1. Construct a map of the Middle East showing the journeys of Abraham. This could be a flour and salt map.

2. Make a three dimensional mural of Abraham's response to God.

3. Gather information about the places visited by Abraham during his journeys. Conduct a pretend trip through this same area with members of the class acting as guides.

4. Make a tabletop scene depicting the life and times of Abraham.

Genesis

Teacher's Outline

THE BOOK OF GENESIS

LESSON #6, THE PROMISE OF A SON TO ABRAHAM

PASSAGE TO STUDY: Genesis 15:1-18:15

SUGGESTIONS FOR SCRIPTURES TO BE READ IN CLASS
Basic	Supplementary
Genesis 15:1-6	Romans 4:1-25
Genesis 17:1-8	Galatians 3:6-9,15-18,23-29
Genesis 18:1-15	

SCRIPTURE MEMORY FOR OCTOBER
  Romans 3:23, "since all have sinned and fall short of the glory of God,..."

BASIC CONCEPTS
1. God's methods contrasted with human methods: the ways of the Spirit contrasted with the ways of the flesh. God wants us to trust in him. He wants us to believe that he will provide things for us that we do not yet see.

2. The principle of the covenant: God wants us to depend upon his promises. See especially Genesis 15:12-21.

3. Salvation by faith is illustrated and upheld by Abraham's response to God's promise. Because he believed the Lord, God imputed righteousness to him (Genesis 15:6).

4. Circumcision was a sign that God gave to Abraham and his descendants as a sign of God's covenant with Abraham (Genesis 17:9-14).

GOALS
1. To better understand what it means to believe in God and commit oneself to him

2. To be able to identify the basic promises that God has given to Abraham

DISCUSSION QUESTIONS
1. Why did God let Abraham and Sarah wait so long for the son of promise?

GREEN LEAF BIBLE SERIES

    2. What did God do to help Abraham become a man of faith?

    3. What did God promise to Abraham?

    4. Why was it difficult for Sarah to believe?

PROJECTS
1. Make a list: either by each individual writing one or through group discussion of some of the things that God wants us to trust him for that are not yet realized.

2. List the basic items of the covenant that God has made with Abraham.

Genesis

Teacher's Outline

THE BOOK OF GENESIS

LESSON #7, THE SAVING OF LOT

PASSAGE TO STUDY: Genesis 18:16-21:34

SUGGESTIONS FOR SCRIPTURE TO BE READ IN CLASS
    Basic   Supplementary
    Genesis 19:1-11   Luke 17:28-32
    Genesis 19:15-28   Romans 1:26-32
    Genesis 21:1-14   II Peter 2:6-10

SCRIPTURE MEMORY FOR OCTOBER
    Romans 3:23, "since all have sinned and fall short of the glory of God,..."

BASIC CONCEPTS
1. The judgment of God and the grace of God are both illustrated in the divine dialogue with Abraham regarding Sodom and Gomorrah and God's willingness to spare Sodom if even ten righteous persons are found there.

2. People have disturbing and even inconceivable capacities for wickedness, hostility, and indifference to God.

3. God will inevitably judge wickedness with great thoroughness.

4. God's great grace and mercy are displayed in that he saves those who are unworthy of his salvation (Lot and his daughters).

5. The birth of Isaac illustrates the provision of God for those who put their trust in the Lord.

GOALS
1. To understand the working out of God's covenant with Abraham in the preservation of Lot and the birth of Isaac

2. To compare Abraham and Lot, and understand how people frequently create their own spiritual difficulties

3. To understand that the grace of God and his judgment are not contradictory principles

GREEN LEAF BIBLE SERIES

DISCUSSION QUESTIONS
1. How did Abraham acquire his knowledge of God so that he could appeal to the righteousness of God regarding Sodom. See especially Genesis 18:25.

2. What does Genesis 19:1-14 tell us about the character of the people of Sodom?

3. What was Lot's most basic spiritual problem?

4. What was the basic spiritual problem of Lot's wife?

5. Why did Sarah banish Hagar and Ishmael?

PROJECTS
1. Have someone report on attempts to excavate or find the cities of Sodom and Gomorrah.

2. Make a list of the times that angels visited people in the Old Testament.

3. Learn some of the things that the Old Testament has to say about the Moabites and the Ammonites (Genesis 19:36-38).

4. Make a list of the people that God provides for and ways that he provides for them in Genesis 19, 20, and 21.

Genesis

Teacher's Outline

THE BOOK OF GENESIS

LESSON #8, THE GREAT TEST OF ABRAHAM

PASSAGE TO STUDY: Genesis 22:1-25:18

SUGGESTIONS FOR SCRIPTURE TO BE READ IN CLASS
<u>Basic</u>   <u>Supplementary</u>
Genesis 22:1-14   II Chronicles 3:1 (Mount Moriah)
Genesis 24:1-27   Micah 6:6,7
                                II Kings 16:2ff
                                Romans 4:16-21
                                I Corinthians 7:12-16
                                II Corinthians 6:14-18
                                Hebrews 11:17-19
                                Hebrews 6:13-15
                                Jeremiah 7:31

SCRIPTURE MEMORY FOR OCTOBER
    Romans 3:23, "since all have sinned and fall short of the glory of God,..."

BASIC CONCEPTS
1. God's commandment to Abraham to present Isaac as an offering is consistent with the first commandment (Exodus 20:3) in that nothing is to be given priority over God.

2. Salvation and the principle of sacrifice: the ram caught in the thicket offered instead of Isaac is a type of Jesus Christ. Isaac was spared, but God did not spare himself seeing his son to the cross.

3. God has a will and purpose for human marriage. Those who believe in God should marry others of like faith.

GOALS
1. To understand that we are to love and worship God first. No person or thing is to have priority over God in our lives

2. To understand that faith in God involves personal commitment

3. To understand that the will of God involves basic decisions in our lives including the person that we marry and the vocation that we pursue

GREEN LEAF BIBLE SERIES

DISCUSSION QUESTIONS
1. Can you think of other instances when God made difficult requests of people that required great faith?

2. Why did Abraham insist on buying the field and the cave of Machpelah? Why did he not accept it as a gift

3. Why did Abraham's servant want to return with Rebekah without any delay?

4. What do we learn about marriage in the account regarding Isaac and Rebekah?

PROJECTS
1. Make a genealogical chart showing the descendants of Terah. Begin with Genesis 11:27-30.

2. Do a study of the Hittites (Genesis 23).

3. Prepare puppets that can be used for presenting the story of Isaac's marriage, and can be adapted for future lessons.

4. Make a chronology of Abraham's life listing his age at the major events in his life.

Genesis

Teacher's Outline

THE BOOK OF GENESIS

LESSON #9, ISAAC AND JACOB

PASSAGE TO STUDY: Genesis 25:19-27:45

SUGGESTIONS FOR SCRIPTURE TO BE READ IN CLASS
<table>
<tr><td>Basic</td><td>Supplementary</td></tr>
<tr><td>Genesis 25:19-26</td><td>Psalms 105:7-11</td></tr>
<tr><td>Genesis 26:1-5</td><td>Hebrews 11:20,21</td></tr>
<tr><td>Genesis 27:1-29</td><td>Hebrews 12:16,17</td></tr>
<tr><td></td><td>James 2:21,22</td></tr>
</table>

SCRIPTURE MEMORY FOR NOVEMBER
II Timothy 2:15, "Do your best to present yourself to God as one approved, a workman who has no need to be ashamed, rightly handling the word of truth."

BASIC CONCEPTS
1. The covenant that God established with Abraham is continued through Isaac and Jacob.

2. God providentially cares for Isaac and his family in provision of children through Rebekah, provision of places to dwell, in the great prosperity that he bestows upon Isaac, and even in the outcome of the rivalry between Jacob and Esau.

3. Parents need to be evenhanded and honest in their relationships with their children.

4. Dishonest behavior makes life much more difficult and brings most unwelcome consequences.

GOALS
1. To be able to identify Abraham, Sarah, Isaac, Hagar, Ishmael, Rebekah, Jacob, and Esau

2. To understand that God keeps his promises and continues his purposes, and that we can trust in him

DISCUSSION QUESTIONS
1. Did Jacob deal wrongly with Easu in purchasing his birthright?

GREEN LEAF BIBLE SERIES

    2. Was Esau at fault regarding the matter of the birthright?

    3. Why was the blessing of Isaac important to Jacob?

    4. How could God's will for Isaac and his sons have been carried out without the trickery and deception of Jacob and his mother?

PROJECTS
1. Discuss the attitudes of Isaac and Rebekah toward their children and the consequences of those attitudes.

2. Discuss Esau and Jacob. List their strong and weak points.

3. Have students draw pictures of what they think Jacob and Esau looked like.

4. Explore and list the characteristics of Isaac from such passages as Genesis 24:62-67; 26:17-25; 26:26-31.

5. Play a game of charades to help accomplish Goal 1.

6. Read Genesis 27 as a drama with four characters and a narrator.

7. Discuss the ways in which individuals let the possibility of immediate pleasure keep them from a goal that is much more worthwhile.

Genesis

Teacher's Outline

THE BOOK OF GENESIS

LESSON #10, JACOB IN THE HOUSEHOLD OF LABAN

PASSAGE TO STUDY: Genesis 27:46-30:43

SUGGESTIONS FOR SCRIPTURE TO BE READ IN CLASS

Basic	Supplementary
Genesis 27:46-28:5	Matthew 8:11
Genesis 28:10-22	John 4:5-12
Genesis 29:1-12	Hebrews 11:20,21
	John 1:51
	John 14:6

SCRIPTURE MEMORY FOR NOVEMBER
  II Timothy 2:15, "Do your best to present yourself to God as one approved, a workman who has no need to be ashamed, rightly handling the word of truth."

BASIC CONCEPTS
1. Jacob's encounter with God at Bethel: God's reaffirmation of his covenant with Abraham and Isaac to Jacob. Jacob's commitment to God.

2. The line of faith and salvation continues to unfold according to God's purpose rather than by man's strategy.

3. Jacob experiences the same dishonest treatment from Laban that Jacob had accorded Esau. Galatians 6:7, "for whatever a man sows that he will also reap."

4. Jacob's vision of the ladder teaches that earth and heaven are linked, and that there is constant commerce between them.

5. The principle of the tithe
    a. Genesis 14:20
    b. Genesis 14:22-99
    c. Genesis 27:30-33
    d. Genesis 28:22
    e. Malachi 3:10

6. The end does not justify the means.

GREEN LEAF BIBLE SERIES

GOALS
1. To understand God's commitment to a group of people through whom he will reach and save the world

2. To see Jacob's underlying commitment to the purposes of God in spite of his many weaknesses

3. To understand that real happiness is based on truthfulness and straightforwardness

DISCUSSION QUESTIONS
1. Why did Jacob leave his home to go to Paddan-aram?

2. What do you see as the significance of God's appearance to Jacob at Bethel?

3. What basic character problem did Laban have?

4. What character strengths do you see in Jacob?

PROJECTS
1. Prepare a map illustrating Jacob's journey from his homeland to Laban's household (and use also in connection with Lessons #11 and #12.

2. Prepare a poster with pictures of scenes that may have been familiar to Jacob. National Geographic magazines might be helpful.

3. Discuss Genesis 28:10-17 in connection with the song, "We Are Climbing Jacob's Ladder."

4. Continue to list the strong and weak points of Jacob.

5. Prepare a "This Is Your Life" television program about Jacob, possibly using a tape recorder.

6. Prepare a new broadcast of Genesis 27:41-28:22 combining interviews with participants and observations on their actions.

7. Discuss situational opportunities for truthfulness and straightforwardness on the student's level. Use role playing to develop situations and actions.

Genesis

Teacher's Outline

THE BOOK OF GENESIS

LESSON #11, JACOB'S RETURN TO CANAAN

PASSAGE TO STUDY: Genesis 31:1-36:43

SUGGESTIONS FOR SCRIPTURE TO BE READ IN CLASS
   Basic
   Genesis 31:1-16
   Genesis 32:9-12
   Genesis 32:22-32
   Genesis 33:1-11

SCRIPTURE MEMORY FOR NOVEMBER
   II Timothy 2:15, "Do your best to present yourself to God as one approved, a workman who has no need to be ashamed, rightly handling the word of truth."

BASIC CONCEPTS
   1. God's covenant with Abraham, Isaac, and Jacob continues to unfold in the departure of Jacob from Paddan-aram and his return to Canaan.

   2. God rewards those who seek his blessing. See especially Genesis 32:24-29.

   3. We should make great effort to get along with people. Note Jacob's attempt to make peace with Esau, first sending messengers ahead of him to Esau and then sending several generous gifts spaced in such a way as to gain the most favorable disposition from Esau. The following passages have to do with the idea of getting along with people:
      a. Proverbs 15:1
      b. Proverbs 16:7
      c. Proverbs 17:9
      d. Proverbs 17:14
      e. Proverbs 20:3
      f. Romans 12:14-21
      g. Matthew 5:43-47

   4. Every person needs to make definite responses to God. Jacob builds altars and places of worship as memorials that God has spoken and as reminders of his response.
      a. Genesis 28:18,19
      b. Genesis 31:13

GREEN LEAF BIBLE SERIES

    c. Genesis 32:30-32
    d. Genesis 33:20
    e. Genesis 35:1
    f. Genesis 35:9-15

GOALS
1. To encourage the making of specific commitments to God

2. To further understand Jacob's underlying commitment to spiritual realities

DISCUSSION QUESTIONS
1. Why did Rachel take the household gods from her father?

2. What is the significance or value of the pillar, "Mizpah?"

3. Was Jacob fair or unfair in his dealings with Laban?

4. Did Jacob handle his meeting with Esau in the right manner? What would you have done differently?

5. What do we learn about Jacob in the encounter with the angel?

6. What do we learn about God in this episode?

PROJECTS
1. Discuss basic commitments that have been made or that we may be ready to make with God.

2. Continue the map work illustrating Jacob's return from Paddanaram to Canaan.

3. Draw pictures showing the meeting of Jacob and Esau.

4. Do a study of Jacob tracing his spiritual growth.

5. Discuss forgiveness in connection with brother and sister relationships.

6. Have each student make a personal spiritual coat-of-arms. Have some sample coats-of-arms on display as models.

Genesis

Teacher's Outline

THE BOOK OF GENESIS

LESSON #12, THE STORY OF JOSEPH

PASSAGE TO STUDY: Genesis 37:1-50:26

SUGGESTIONS FOR SCRIPTURE TO BE READ IN CLASS
<table>
<tr><td>Basic</td><td>Supplementary</td></tr>
<tr><td>Genesis 37:1-11</td><td>Exodus 1:5-8</td></tr>
<tr><td>Genesis 39:1-6</td><td>Exodus 13:19</td></tr>
<tr><td>Genesis 40:1-23</td><td>Joshua 24:32</td></tr>
<tr><td>Genesis 41:1-45</td><td></td></tr>
<tr><td>Genesis 42:1-17</td><td></td></tr>
<tr><td>Genesis 45:1-9</td><td></td></tr>
</table>

SCRIPTURE MEMORY FOR NOVEMBER
II Timothy 2:15, "Do your best to present youself to God as one approved, a workman who has no need to be ashamed, rightly handling the word of truth."

BASIC CONCEPTS
1. Joseph is an excellent example of a person of faith and obedience. He is a good model for believers to emulate.

2. Patience is an important biblical principle. God has abundant rewards for those who wait on him.

3. Egypt was the greatest nation in the world at the time of Jacob and Joseph.

4. The Bible places great emphasis on forgiveness and avoiding resentment. Joseph illustrates both qualities.

GOALS
1. Students should be able to retell the accounts of Abraham, Isaac, Jacob, and Joseph, in broad terms, in their own words. This might provide the basis for a quiz. See Lesson #13.

2. To better comprehend the dangers of jealousy and animosity, and the strength of forgiveness

GREEN LEAF BIBLE SERIES

DISCUSSION QUESTIONS
1. Why did Joseph tell his family about his dreams? Why didn't he keep them to himself?

2. Why were Joseph's brothers so deeply offended by his dreams?

3. What qualities do you think brought Joseph to prominence in Potiphar's household and then even in prison?

4. Why in God's providence did Joseph rise to such a position of importance in Egypt?

5. Why did Joseph put his brothers through various trials?

6. What is the most valuable character trait exhibited by Joseph?

PROJECTS
1. Discuss Joseph's attitude toward his brothers and his treatment of them when they came to Egypt. Why did he treat them roughly? Why did he forgive them?

2. Prepare a poster with pictures (and perhaps, other information) depicting Egypt during the time of Joseph.

3. Use role playing to act out situations of jealousy, animosity, and the spoiled child.

Genesis

Teacher's Outline

THE BOOK OF GENESIS

LESSON #13: QUIZ

1. What pattern did God use when he made man? _____
   _____

2. What is the relationship of man to the creation? _____
   _____

3. From what do we derive the idea of a day of rest and worship? ___
   _____

4. Name the three sons of Adam and Eve: 1) _____
   2) _____   3) _____

5. What happened to the first son of Adam and Eve? _____
   _____

6. Which son represents the line of "godly purpose"? _____
   _____

7. What means did God use to save Noah and his family? _____
   _____

8. What was a visible sign of God's covenant with Noah? _____
   _____

9. Name the three sons of Noah: 1) _____
   2) _____   3) _____

10. Which of Noah's sons represents the line of "godly purpose"? _____
    _____

11. Where was Abraham born? _____

12. To what town in northern Mesopotamia did Abraham move? _____
    _____

13. What land did God lead Abraham to? _____

GREEN LEAF BIBLE SERIES

14. What was the name of Abraham's wife? _____

15. Name Abraham's nephew, who accompanied him: _____

16. Where did this nephew finally settle? _____

17. What was the name of the son God promised to Abraham and his wife? _____

18. What was the name of the son's wife? _____

19. Where was she from? _____

20. Name their two sons: 1) _____ 2) _____

21. What two important things did Jacob "wrest" from his brother Esau?
    1) _____
    2) _____

22. What were two reasons for Isaac and Rebekah sending Jacob to Paddan-aram?
    1) _____
    2) _____

23. What were the names of Jacob's two wives? 1) _____
    2) _____

24. How many sons did Jacob have? _____

25. What were the names of the two favorite sons? 1) _____
    2) _____

26. About how long was Jacob with Laban in Paddan-aram? _____

27. What "spiritual" event happened to Jacob before he met Esau? ____
    _____

28. Esau became the father of what nation? _____

29. What happened to Joseph when he was 17 years old? _____
    _____

30. Why did Jacob and his family move to Egypt? _____
    _____

Genesis

31. What were the names of Joseph's two sons? 1) _____
    2) _____

HEROES OF THE BIBLE

Unit Two   The Gospel of Luke
17 Weeks

GREEN LEAF BIBLE SERIES

YEAR ONE, UNIT TWO

THE GOSPEL OF LUKE

Week One	INTRODUCTION
	    Differences between the Gospels
	    Overview of the life of Christ
	    Prologue
		Luke 1:1-4

Week Two	PREPARATION FOR THE BIRTH OF JESUS	Luke 1:5-80
Week Three	THE BIRTH AND EARLY YEARS OF JESUS	Luke 2:1-52
Week Four	JOHN THE BAPTIST THE BEGINNING OF JESUS' MINISTRY	Luke 3:1-4:41
Week Five	INITIAL PREACHING OF THE GOOD NEWS THE APPOINTMENT OF THE DISCIPLES	Luke 4:42-6:49
Week Six	MARVELOUS HEALINGS SEVERAL SIGNIFICANT EVENTS	Luke 7:1-8:56
Week Seven	JESUS AS THE DIVINE SON	Luke 9:10-62
Week Eight	JESUS' COMMISSIONINGS OF HIS DISCIPLES TO WITNESS	Luke 9:1-9 10:1-24; 24:44-53
Week Nine	A TRUE RELATIONSHIP TO GOD	Luke 10:25-11:52
Week Ten	KEYS TO DISCIPLESHIP I	Luke 11:53-13:30
Week Eleven	KEYS TO DISCIPLESHIP II	Luke 13:31-14:35

Week Twelve	THREE PARABLES ON THE LOVE OF GOD
	    The lost sheep
	    The lost coin
	    The lost son
		Luke 15:1-32

Week Thirteen	TEACHINGS ON COMMITMENT	Luke 16:1-17:19

Luke

Week Fourteen	TEACHINGS AND INCIDENTS ON THE WAY TO JERUSALEM	Luke 17:20-19:27
Week Fifteen	TRIUMPHAL ENTRY AND FINAL DISCOURSES	Luke 19:28-21:38
Week Sixteen	FINAL EVENTS/CRUCIFIXION RESURRECTION AND CONSUMMATION	Luke 22:1-24:43

GREEN LEAF BIBLE SERIES

THE BOOK OF LUKE

CURRICULUM RESOURCE LIST   APPROXIMATE PRICE

BOOKS
Luke's Story of Jesus, O.C. Edwards, Jr.; Fortress   3.95
   (available from Cokesbury)
Pocket Size Portions: Luke; American Bible Society   .15
My Jesus Book, Wanda Hayes; Standard   4.95
If You Lived in Bible Times, Nancy Williamson; Victor Books   6.95
Arch Books; Concordia   .79
   "The Secret Journey"
   "The Unforgiving Servant"
   "The Happiest Search"
   "Eight Bags of Gold"
   "The Boy Who Ran Away"
   "The Baby God Promised"
   "Jesus and the Stranger"
   "The Fisherman's Surprise"
   "Jesus' Second Family"
   "The Rich Fool"
Tell-A-Bible-Story Book; Standard   .79
   "Jesus Is Born"
   "Wise Men Visit Jesus"
   "Jesus and the Crippled Man"
   "Jesus Feeds 5000"
   "Zaccheus Meets Jesus"
Bible Story Cartoons, Norman Lynch; Standard   .59
   The New Testament, Books 17 through 23 include:
     "The Birth of Jesus"
     "Lost in the Temple"
     "The Devil in the Desert"
     "The Great Catch"
     "Perilous Journey"
     "Jairus' Daughter"
     "Feeding the 5000"
     "Fear in the Night"
     "Miracle on the Mountain"
Meet Jesus, Knofel Staton; Standard   2.95
Bible Stories for Children (stories from Luke); Ideals   3.25

MAPS, CHARTS, TIMELINES
Study Chart of the Life of Jesus; Standard   4.50

TRANSPARENCIES, DUPLICATING MASTERS, FILMSTRIPS, FILMS
"It Began in Bethlehem", filmstrip; Concordia   9.75
   Filmstrip and record   14.25

Luke

The Living Bible Series: Life of Jesus, including John the
    Baptist; Concordia
    22 Filmstrips and 7 Records   137.00
    Filmstrips alone   114.50
    Individual Filmstrips   5.75
    Individual Records   4.25
American Bible Society Films   Purchase   40.00
                                              Rental   7.50
    "The Good Neighbor" (The Good Samaritan)
    "The Happy Man" (healing of the man who could not walk)
    "A Baby Named Jesus"
    "A Runaway Comes Home" (The Prodigal Son)
    "Hosanna Day" (Palm Sunday)
    "It is Written" (Crucifixion and Resurrection)
    "Afraid of the Storm" (calming of the sea)
    "The Cheat Who Changed" (Zaccheus)
Transparencies for Overhead Projectors; Standard
    (each book contains 8 color transparencies, resource
    material, and worksheet spirit masters)
        "The Ministry of Christ"   8.95
        "The Messiah Has Come"   7.95
        "Jesus' Parables of Christian Life"   7.95

FLANNELGRAPH, POSTERS, PICTURES

Suede-Graph; Scripture Press   2.75
    Miracles on the Sea
    Jesus Dies and Lives
    The Prodigal Son
        Casettes available for the above   4.25
Pictograph; Standard   4.50
    Early Life of Jesus
    Later Life of Jesus
    Parables of Jesus
    Miracles of Jesus
Annie Vallotton Posters; American Bible Society   4.00
    (line drawings from the good News Bible, set of 12)
Life of Jesus: Teaching Pictures, Richard and Frances Hook;
    (available from David C. Cook)
        Birth, Boyhood, Early Ministry (12 pictures)
        While Jesus was in Galilee (10 pictures)
        Journey Toward Jerusalem (11 pictures)
        Jesus is Our King (8 pictures)
    Picture sets   6.95
    Slide sets   10.95
    All four picture sets   24.95
    All four slide sets   40.95

GREEN LEAF BIBLE SERIES

ACTIVITY BOOKS, PROJECTS, GAMES, PUZZLES

Bible Time Activity Books; David C. Cook	1.99
Ministry of Christ I	
Ministry of Christ II	
Workbook on the Four Gospels; Standard	3.50
Bible Dioramas; Standard	3.95
If You Had Been Born in Bethlehem, Carol Femtheil	
Make Your Own Nativity Scene; David C. Cook	3.95
Land of Jesus Jigsaw Puzzle; Scripture Press	2.75
My Bible Story Jigsaw Puzzles; David C. Cook	.75
Jesus and the Lost Sheep	
A Walk With Jesus	
Jesus the Shepherd	
Bible Game Chest; David C. Cook	3.50
New Testament Bible Stencils; David C. Cook	2.60

THE GOSPEL OF LUKE

Author: Luke, Physician and companion of Paul, who wrote the two-volume work, Luke-Acts. Tradition consistently assigns the book to Luke and this corresponds with internal evidence in the letters of Paul and book of Acts. "...it was part of a decided tendency to ascribe the writing of books and epistles to the apostles or to others of the most important eyewitnesses...it would be historically inexplicable why tradition should ascribe the third gospel to Luke if he had not really been the author of it." (Norval Geldenhuys, Commentary on the Gospel of Luke, p. 19.) "...the illustrious German historian Eduard Meyer... declared that Luke must be given a prominent place among the most significant historians of world history." (Geldenhuys, p. 28.)

Date: 60 A.D. This date is harmonious with our understanding that the gospel was written by Luke. It assumes that Luke was written before Acts, and that Acts was written no later than 64 A.D. Otherwise Acts would have mentioned subsequent events in Paul's life.

Place of Writing: Caesarea during the period of the Apostle Paul's imprisonment in that city.

Purpose: To give a concise and organized account of the ministry of Jesus Christ in the Greek historical tradition. Luke and Acts are written for or dedicated to Theophilus, a person of some prominence. However, the gospel was undoubtedly written for the entire gentile world.

Characteristics:
1. the nativity narratives
2. an evident awareness of the customs and significance of the Roman Empire
3. the place of women in the ministry of Jesus Christ
4. prayer
5. Jesus' dealings with gentiles
6. the development or unfolding of the ministry and life of Jesus. Luke's primary concern seems to be to reveal the person of Jesus Christ rather than follow a strict chronological arrangement. The general arrangement is as follows: the annunciation, birth, childhood, human development, God's approval at the temptation, leadership ability, authority over all sorts of diseases, the announcement of a new order, appointment of disciples, relationships of prayer with the Father, new teachings, fulfillment of messianic purposes, and final commissioning of the disciples.

OUTLINE OF LUKE
    I.   PROLOGUE (1:1-4)

    II.   PREPARATION AND EARLY YEARS OF JESUS (1:5-3:38)

GREEN LEAF BIBLE SERIES

      1.   The announcement of the forerunner (1:5-25)

      2.   The announcement of the Messiah (1:26-56)
           a.   Gabriel announces to Mary that she is to bear the son of the Most High God (1:26-38)
           b.   Elizabeth blesses Mary (1:39-45)
           c.   Mary's response [The Magnificat] (1:46-55)
           d.   the duration of Mary's stay with Elizabeth (1:56)

      3.   The birth of John the Baptist (1:57-80)
           a.   the birth and naming of the child (1:57-66)
           b.   Zechariah prophesies (1:67-80)

      4.   The birth and early years of the Christ (2:1-52)
           a.   the trip to Bethlehem (2:1-7)
           b.   angelic announcement of the birth to shepherds (2:8-21)
           c.   the fulfillment of the requirements of the Jewish law (2:22-40)
           d.   the trip to Jerusalem at the age of twelve (2:41-52)

      5.   John the Baptist (3:1-22)
           a.   the beginning of his ministry (3:1-3)
           b.   prophecy fulfilled (3:4-6)
           c.   a synopsis of his ministry (3:7-20)
           d.   the baptism of Jesus (3:21,22)

      6.   The ancestry of Jesus (3:23-38)

III.   THE MINISTRY OF JESUS CHRIST (4:1-19:27)
      1.   The temptation of Jesus (4:1-13)

      2.   Jesus' fame spreads (4:14,15)

      3.   He is rejected by the people of his own town (4:16-30)

      4.   Some examples of his healing ministry and authority over evil spirits (4:31-41)

      5.   Initial preaching of the good news of the kingdom of God (4:42-6:11)
           a.   Jesus preaches in the synagogues of Judea (4:42-44)
           b.   a great catch of fish and of men (5:1-11)
           c.   a leper is healed (5:12-16)
           d.   Jesus heals a paralyzed man that is let down through the roof (5:17-26)
           e.   the call of Levi (5:27-32)
           f.   the new order of Jesus Christ (5:33-39)
           g.   the question of Sabbath observance (6:1-11)

Luke

6. The appointment of the disciples and related events (6:12-49)
    a. the official appointment of the disciples (6:12-16)
    b. a great crowd gathers and Jesus heals many (6:17-19)
    c. the ordination sermon (6:20-49)

7. Healing and teaching (7:1-8:56)
    a. Jesus heals the slave of a centurion (7:1-10)
    b. Jesus raises the son of a widow (7:11-17)
    c. John sends a question to Jesus (7:18-23)
    d. Jesus points out the inconsistency of those who reject both him and John (7:24-35)
    e. Jesus forgives a sinful woman (7:36-50)
    f. women who aided Jesus in his ministry (8:1-3)
    g. parable of the sower (8:4-18)
    h. Jesus' true family (8:19-32)
    i. the storm rebuked (8:22-25)
    j. the healing of the Gerasene demoniac (8:26-39)
    k. a woman healed (8:43-48)
    l. Jairus' daughter raised from dead (8:40-42,49-56)

8. Further accounts regarding the person of Jesus and his relations with the disciples (9:1-10:24)
    a. the twelve sent forth to preach and heal (9:1-6)
    b. Herod takes note of this extraordinary ministry (9:7-9)
    c. a multitude is miraculously fed (9:10-17)
    d. Peter declares Jesus to be the Messiah (9:18-22)
    e. Jesus sets forth requirements of discipleship (9:23-27)
    f. the transfiguration (9:28-36)
    g. several instances illustrating the weaknesses of the disciples (9:37-56)
        1) Jesus heals a boy the disciples could not heal (9:37-43a)
        2) they failed to understand his teaching about the end of his ministry (9:43b-45)
        3) they argued among themselves as to which of them was the greatest (9:46-48)
        4) they evidenced intolerance toward others who were serving Jesus (9:49,50)
        5) they showed excessive zeal for vengeance (9:51-56)
    h. further emphases on the requirements of discipleship (9:57-62)
    i. appointment of the seventy and their triumph (10:1-24)

9. Some teachings about a true relationship to God (10:25-11:52)
    a. a lawyer's question: parable of the good Samaritan (10:25-42)
    b. prayer (11:1-13)
    c. evil spirits (11:14-26)

GREEN LEAF BIBLE SERIES

      d. God's blessings are not received through family relationships but through hearing and doing God's word (11:27,28)
      e. only one sign to be given to this generation (11:29-32)
      f. the spiritual importance of the eye (11:33-36)
      g. the Pharisees are an example of an outward religion without an inward reality (11:37-44)
      h. Jesus exposes the false religion of the lawyers (11:45-52)

10. Concluding teaching and increasing conflict (11:53-14:6)
      a. Scribes and Pharisees try to trap Jesus (11:53,54)
      b. brief statements and parables regarding the final reckoning (12:1-13:9)
      c. an infirm woman healed on the Sabbath (13:10-17)
      d. two short parables about the kingdom of God (13:18-21)
      e. concerning those who will be saved (13:22-30)
      f. Jesus speaks of his coming death (13:31-35)
      g. another healing on the Sabbath (14:1-6)

11. Additional instructions about man's relationship to God (14:7-17:18)
      a. the importance of humility (14:7-11)
      b. the importance of giving without expecting to receive (14:12-14)
      c. the supreme importance of God's invitation (14:15-24)
      d. discipleship requires complete dedication (14:25-35)
      e. three parables illustrating the persevering love of God (15:1-32)
          1) the lost sheep (15:3-7)
          2) the lost coin (15:8-10)
          3) the lost son (15:11-32)
      f. God expects us to make wise use of what has been entrusted to us (16:1-13)
      g. Jesus admonishes the Pharisees that God's true law must be kept (16:14-18)
      h. a parable illustrating the importance of appropriating the present opportunity with God (16:19-31)
      i. God requires that we be a means to helping others, not a cause of their falling (17:1-4)
      j. the power of faith (17:5,6)
      k. the servant of the Lord should not think well of himself because he has obeyed (17:7-10)
      l. ten lepers healed: an example of gratitude to God (17:11-19)

12. Miscellaneous teachings and incidents (17:20-19:27)
      a. teachings related to the advent of the kingdom of God (17:20-37)
      b. teaching on prayer (18:1-14)

Luke

              1) the widow and the unrighteous judge (18:1-8)
              2) the Pharisee and the tax collector (18:9-14)
       c. Jesus asks that the infants be brought to him (18:15-17)
       d. Jesus and the rich ruler (19:18-30)
       e. Jesus foretells his suffering (18:31-34)
       f. Jesus heals a blind beggar on the road to Jericho (18:35-43)
       g. Jesus dines with Zacchaeus (19:1-10)
       h. parable of the nobleman and ten servants (19:11-27)

IV. CLIMAX AND CONSUMMATION (19:28-24:53)

    1. The triumphal entry into Jerusalem (19:28-48)

    2. Final discourses (20:1-21:38)
       a. some difficult questions are put to Jesus (20:1-47)
          1) regarding the source of his authority (20:1-18)
          2) loyalty to God or Caesar? (20:19-26)
          3) regarding marriage (20:27-40)
          4) Jesus responds with a question (20:41-47)
       b. Jesus emphasizes the principle of sacrifice in giving (21:1-4)
       c. Jesus speaks of the end of the age (21:5-38)

    3. Final fellowship with the disciples (22:1-46)
       a. the last supper (22:1-22:38)
       b. at the Mount of Olives (22:39-46)

    4. Arrest, trial, and crucifixion (22:47-23:56)
       a. the arrest (22:47-53)
       b. Peter's denials (22:54-62)
       c. the trials of Jesus (22:63-23:25)
          1) before the Jewish council (22:63-71)
          2) before Pilate (23:1-5)
          3) before Herod (23:6-12)
          4) final sentencing before Pilate (23:13-25)
       d. the crucifixion (23:26-49)
       e. the burial (23:50-56)

    5. The consummation (24:1-53)
       a. the open tomb (24:1-11)
       b. Jesus talks with two disciples on the road to Emmaus (24:12-32)
       c. the complete fulfillment of scripture and the final commissioning (24:33-53)

GREEN LEAF BIBLE SERIES

Teacher's Outline

THE GOSPEL OF LUKE

LESSON #1, INTRODUCTION

PASSAGE TO STUDY: Luke 1:1-4

SUGGESTIONS FOR SCRIPTURE TO BE READ IN CLASS
- Basic
- Luke 1:1-4

- Supplementary
- Acts 1:1,2
- John 20:30,31

MEMORY VERSE FOR DECEMBER
Luke 2:52, "And Jesus increased in wisdom and in stature, and in favor with God and man."

BASIC CONCEPTS
1. Luke is a two-volume work: Luke and Acts written by Luke, physician and a close associate of the Apostle Paul.

2. The gospels derive from the proclamation of the apostles and the early church about Jesus, the Messiah.
    a. not biography in the strict sense
    b. written from different perspectives--regard for the personalities and viewpoints of the authors

3. The reliability of the gospels.
    a. their consistency
    b. the character and credibility of the men who wrote them
    c. Luke's testimony as to his own care in this undertaking (1:2,3)

4. The distinction between the Synoptics and the fourth gospel

GOALS
1. Be able to identify the four gospels and their authors

2. To understand the basic purposes of the gospels
    a. proclamation about Christ to the end that people may believe (see John 20:30,31)
    b. highly selective in their use of material

3. To understand the reliability of the gospels

Luke

4. To have an overview of the life of Christ

DISCUSSION QUESTIONS
1. What made Luke especially able or qualified to write one of the gospels?

2. How well do the gospels cover what you would like to know about Jesus?

PROJECTS
1. Establish criteria for determining the reliability of the accounts regarding Julius Caesar or George Washington. Can these criteria be applied to the account regarding Jesus Christ?

2. Have a series of pictures depicting Jesus' life and a series of corresponding verses. Have students match pictures and verses. Place pictures in chronological order.

3. Prepare individual maps of Palestine to be completed as an ongoing project throughout the study.

4. Begin a timeline of the life of Jesus to be illustrated with drawings and cut out pictures as an ongoing project.

GREEN LEAF BIBLE SERIES

THE GOSPEL OF LUKE

LESSON #1: Supplementary Material

A. Differences between the gospels
   1. The Synoptics: Matthew, Mark, Luke
      a. parables and brief teachings
      b. emphasize Jesus' ministry in Galilee
      c. many miracles

   2. The gospel of John
      a. no parables
      b. longer discourses
      c. emphasizes Jesus' ministry in Judea and Jerusalem
      d. fewer miracles: some of which are designated as "signs"

B. General ideas on the sources of the gospels:
   1. Oral tradition

   2. Written records

   3. Two document hypothesis

   4. Four document hypothesis

   5. A recent idea is that each gospel developed from a community that had a particular slant on the ministry of Jesus

C. What were Luke's sources?
   1. Many written records

   2. Eyewitnesses

   3. Personal investigation ("followed all things closely")

   4. An organized account of reliable information ("an orderly account...that you may know the truth...")

D. Luke as the author of the gospel
   1. Not mentioned by name in Luke or Acts

   2. References to Luke in the New Testament
      a. Colossians 4:14, "Luke the beloved physician and Demas greet you."
      b. II Timothy 4:10,11, "For Demas, in love with this present world, has deserted me and gone to Thessalonica; Crescens has gone to Galatia, Titus to Dalmatia. Luke alone is with

Luke

      me. Get Mark and bring him with you; for he is very useful in serving me."
- c. Philemon 23,24, "Epaphras, my fellow prisoner in Christ Jesus, sends greetings to you, and so do Mark, Aristarchus, Demas, and Luke, my fellow workers."
- d. Acts, "we" passages (Acts 16:10 and following)

GREEN LEAF BIBLE SERIES

THE GOSPEL OF LUKE

LESSON #2, PREPARATION FOR THE BIRTH OF JESUS

PASSAGE TO STUDY: Luke 1:5-80

SUGGESTIONS FOR SCRIPTURE TO BE READ IN CLASS
   Basic
   Luke 1:5-23
   Luke 1:26-38
   Luke 1:39-45
   Luke 1:46-56

   Supplementary
   Malachi 4:5,6
   Isaiah 40:3-5

MEMORY VERSE FOR DECEMBER
   Luke 2:52, "And Jesus increased in wisdom and in stature and in favor with God and man."

BASIC CONCEPTS
1. The outline of the temple and its furnishings.

2. The fulfillment of the word of God to Abraham, Isaac, Jacob, and the prophets in the births of John the Baptist and of Jesus. See Luke 1:33.

3. The importance of faith: the rebuke to Zechariah because he did not fully believe in the words of the Angel. See Luke 1:20.

4. The example of the faith and obedience of Mary. See especially Luke 1:38 and 1:45.

5. Great hope was portended by the births of John the Baptist and of Jesus.
   a. Luke 1:53,54
   b. Luke 1:76-79

GOALS
1. Be able to identify:
   a. Zechariah
   b. Elizabeth
   c. Mary
   d. Joseph
   e. Gabriel
   f. John the Baptist

Luke

2. Geography: Be able to identify and locate Judea, Galilee, Nazareth

3. Understand that the promised birth of Jesus was in fulfillment of the word of God to Abraham, Isaac, Jacob and the prophets

DISCUSSION QUESTIONS
1. What kind of righteousness did Elizabeth and Zechariah exhibit?

2. What positive qualities does Mary exemplify in Luke 1:26-56?

3. What do you think is Mary's most admirable trait or quality?

4. What is the main theme or themes of Zechariah's prophecy in Luke 1:67-79?

PROJECTS
1. Prepare a list of Old Testament passages that refer to the birth or advent of Jesus.

2. Prepare an outline of the Temple and place arrows representing Zechariah and Gabriel in appropriate places.

3. Have students read the passage as a four-part play, using a narrator and the characters of the story.

GREEN LEAF BIBLE SERIES

Teacher's Outline

THE GOSPEL OF LUKE

LESSON #3, THE BIRTH AND EARLY YEARS OF JESUS

PASSAGE TO STUDY: Luke 2:1-52

SUGGESTIONS FOR SCRIPTURE TO BE READ IN CLASS
    Basic   Supplementary
    Luke 2:1-14   Matthew 1:18-25
    Luke 2:15-21   Philippians 2:5-11
    Luke 2:41-52

MEMORY VERSE FOR DECEMBER
    Luke 2:52, "And Jesus increased in wisdom and in stature, and in favor with God and man."

BASIC CONCEPTS
1. The full humanity of Jesus Christ
    a. physical birth
    b. need for the nurture and care of his parents
    c. physical, spiritual, mental, and social growth and development

2. Testimony that this was the Messiah, the Savior of the world
    a. the angelic appearance to Mary (1:26-38)
    b. the angelic appearance to the shepherds and their visit to the manger (2:8-20)
    c. the testimony of Simeon (2:25-35)
    d. the testimony of Anna (2:36-38)

3. Prophecies regarding the Messiah (related to Luke 2:4)
    a. that he was to be of the line of David
        1) II Samuel 7:12,13
        2) II Samuel 7:16
        3) Isaiah 9:6,7
        4) Isaiah 11:1,10
    b. that he was to be born in Bethlehem
        1) Micah 5:2
    c. that he was to be associated with Nazareth
        1) Matthew 2:23 (The Old Testament passage that Matthew was referring to is uncertain, perhaps due to a faulty translation at some point. Some think that Matthew referred to Isaiah 11:1 in the Hebrew.)

Luke

GOALS
1. To appreciate the consistency of the testimony regarding the birth of Jesus Christ
   a. Elizabeth and Zechariah
   b. Mary and Joseph
   c. angelic appearances
   d. Old Testament prophecies
   e. the shepherds
   f. the Magi (Matthew 2:1-12)
   g. the gospels of Matthew and Luke
   h. the entire New Testament

2. To understand something of the governmental-political background of Palestine
   a. Babylonian rule (587-539 B.C.)
   b. Persian rule (539-332 B.C.)
   c. Greek rule (332-164 B.C.)
   d. The Maccabean Period [independence from foreign rule] (164-63 B.C.)
   e. Roman Rule (63 B.C.-638 A.D.)
      1) 63 B.C., Pompey takes Jerusalem
      2) 60-30 B.C., Julius Caesar
      3) 30 B.C.-14 A.D., Octavian (Augustus)
      4) 14-37 A.D., Tiberius
      5) 37-41 A.D., Caligula
   f. Government of Palestine in the New Testament period
      1) Herod the Great, (40-4 B.C.): His kingdom included Palestine, Transjordon, and parts of Lebanon and Syria
      2) On the death of Herod the Great, his kingdom was divided into three sections and ruled by three of his sons:
         Herod Antipas (4 B.C.-39 A.D.) Tetrarch of Galilee (executed John the Baptist)
         Herod Archelaus (4 B.C.-6 A.D.), Tetrarch of Judea
         Herod Philip II (4 B.C.-34 A.D.) Tetrarch of Ituraea
      3) When Herod Archelaus died (6 A.D.) the Romans instituted procurators in Judea by direct appointment
         Coponius (6-10 A.D.)
         M. Ambivius (10-13 A.D.)
         Annius Rufus (13-15 A.D.)
         Valerius Gratus (15-26 A.D.)
         Pontius Pilate (26-36 A.D.)

DISCUSSION QUESTIONS
1. What special significance is there that Joseph was "of the house and lineage of David,"?

GREEN LEAF BIBLE SERIES

    2. What revelation was given to the shepherds?

    3. What were two things that Simeon foresaw coming to pass through Jesus?

    4. To what kind of people did Anna give hope because of the birth of Jesus?

    5. What does Luke 2:52 teach us about Jesus?

PROJECTS
1. Have an oral quiz identifying the people in Luke 1 and 2:

Luke	Gabriel
Theophilus	Joseph
Zechariah	Caesar Agustus
Elizabeth	Simeon
Mary	Anna
John (the Baptist)	

2. Have students read aloud the Old Testament passages listed under Basic Concepts 3a.

3. Have students draw pictures of various scenes from Luke 2:1-18. Trace some scenes onto a ditto with appropriate scripture verse. Run off, color, send to convalescent home.

4. Have each student pretend to be a character from Luke 1 or 2. He tells the events in which he was involved and his relationship to Jesus from his perspective.

5. Discuss with students what Jesus' birth means to <u>each of us</u> and <u>our</u> feelings when we realize the significance of the event (joyous, happy, excited, thankful, full of praise, etc.). Cut out pictures from magazines which reflect these feelings. Mount on butcher paper.

Luke

Teacher's Outline

THE GOSPEL OF LUKE

LESSON #4, JOHN THE BAPTIST
          THE BEGINNING OF JESUS' MINISTRY

PASSAGE TO STUDY: Luke 3:1-4:41

SUGGESTIONS FOR SCRIPTURE TO BE READ IN CLASS
    Basic
    Luke 3:1-9
    Luke 4:1-15
    Luke 4:16-30
    Luke 4:38-41

MEMORY VERSE FOR DECEMBER
    Luke 2:52, "And Jesus increased in wisdom and in stature, and in favor with God and man."

BASIC CONCEPTS
  1. The purpose of the ministry of John the Baptist
     a. to fulfill Old Testament prophecy
     b. to warn people of the need for repentance
     c. to present Jesus as the Messiah
     d. to lay an organizational ground work upon which Jesus began his ministry

  2. John the Baptist clearly taught that a person's belief in God should have a direct impact upon how he lives and relates to others. The person who is out of tune with the purposes of God should repent--making those necessary changes in his life that will bring him into conformity with the will of God. See Luke 3:7-14.

  3. Jesus' identity with us
     a. descended from Adam (3:23-38)
     b. sorely tempted (4:1-13)
     c. misunderstood in his own community (4:22-30)

  4. Jesus spoke with authority and had power to heal. See Luke 4:31-44.

  5. Jesus exercised authority over demons.

GOALS
  1. That each pupil be able to explain the relationship between the

GREEN LEAF BIBLE SERIES

>ministry of John the Baptist and that of Jesus

>2. To learn effective responses to temptation
>   a. obey God
>   b. use the scriptures
>   c. resist the devil

>3. To understand some of the reasons why people may not believe in Jesus

DISCUSSION QUESTIONS
>1. Note the instructions of John the Baptist recorded in Luke 3:10-14. How do they help us understand what repentance means?
>
>2. Why were the people in the synagogue at Nazareth so upset by what Jesus said?
>
>3. Why do we frequently read about direct contact with demons in the four gospels--but almost nowhere else in the Bible? (Acts 16:16-18 is virtually the only exception.)

PROJECTS
>1. Locate the geographic points mentioned in this passage on a map.
>
>2. Discuss the meaning of baptism.
>
>3. Discuss the nature of temptation.
>
>4. Make a list of all New Testament passages referring to John the Baptist.

Luke

Teacher's Outline

THE GOSPEL OF LUKE

LESSON #5, INITIAL PREACHING OF THE GOOD NEWS
THE APPOINTMENT OF THE DISCIPLES

PASSAGE TO STUDY: Luke 4:42-6:49

SUGGESTIONS FOR SCRIPTURE TO BE READ IN CLASS
Basic
Luke 5:1-11
Luke 5:17-26
Luke 6:12-16
Luke 6:20-31

MEMORY VERSE FOR JANUARY
Luke 9:23, "If any man would come after me, let him deny himself and take up his cross daily and follow me."

BASIC CONCEPTS
1. There was a large popular response to the ministry of Jesus
   a. Luke 4:42
   b. Luke 5:1,3
   c. Luke 5:15
   d. Luke 5:19
   e. Luke 6:17

2. Acceptance of Jesus and his teachings requires a break from the past. See Luke 5:36-39.

3. The kingdom of God and the life to come will bring great blessings to those who truly follow Jesus, while those who prosper only in this life will be confounded. See Luke 6:20-26.

4. Love your enemies, and do good to those who hate you. See Luke 6:27-36.

5. It is important to obey Jesus Christ
   a. Luke 5:10,11
   b. Luke 5:27,28
   c. Luke 6:46-49

GOALS
1. To understand the purpose of Jesus' ministry
   a. Luke 4:43

GREEN LEAF BIBLE SERIES

      b. Luke 5:10
      c. Luke 5:20,23-25
      d. Luke 6:17-19
      e. Luke 6:47,48

2. To be able to name the twelve apostles (Luke 6:13-16)

Simon Peter	Matthew
Andrew	Thomas
James	James (the son of Alphaeus)
John	Simon (the Zealot)
Philip	Judas (son of James)
Bartholomew	Judas Iscariot

3. To be able to identify:
   Sea of Galilee (Lake of Genesaret)
   Tyre
   Sidon
   Capernaum
   Jerusalem

DISCUSSION QUESTIONS

1. Is it practicable or possible to follow all of the teachings of Jesus?

2. What was the purpose of Jesus' ministry? See Luke 4:43.

3. What was especially upsetting to the Pharisees in the episode about the healing of the paralyzed man?

4. What did Jesus mean when he said, "new wine must be put into fresh wineskins" (Luke 5:38)?

5. Why did Jesus <u>pointedly</u> heal people on the Sabbath? See Luke 6:6-11.

PROJECTS

1. Prepare a flannelgraph or picture of Jesus teaching the people-- from Simon's boat (Luke 5:3).

2. Have students act out the healing of the paralyzed man (Luke 5:18-26).

3. Ask several of the pupils to explain one each of the beatitudes (Luke 6:20-28).

4. Mark on a map key areas in Goals #3.

Luke

Teacher's Outline

THE GOSPEL OF LUKE

LESSON #6, MARVELOUS HEALINGS/SEVERAL SIGNIFICANT EVENTS
    THE PARABLE OF THE SOWER

PASSAGE TO STUDY: Luke 7:1-8:56

SUGGESTIONS FOR SCRIPTURE TO BE READ IN CLASS

Basic	Supplementary (Relating to Luke
Luke 7:1-10	7:18-23)
Luke 7:11-17	Isaiah 29:18,19
Luke 8:4-15	Isaiah 35:5,6
Luke 8:26-39	Isaiah 61:1

MEMORY VERSE FOR JANUARY
    Luke 9:23, "If any man would come after me, let him deny himself and take up his cross daily and follow me."

BASIC CONCEPTS
1. As the Son of God, Jesus Christ exercised power and authority consistent with that office.
   a. Luke 7:6-9
   b. Luke 7:16
   c. Luke 7:48-50
   d. Luke 8:24,25
   e. Luke 8:26-33
   f. Luke 8:49-56

2. God extends his grace in seeking to win people to himself by various methods. For example see Luke 7:31-35. Note the contrast between John the Baptist and Jesus.

3. Bible study is of basic importance. This principle is illustrated by the parable of the sower (Luke 8:4-15). One of the main devices of the devil is to attempt to keep people from the word of God.

4. The people who respond to Jesus Christ are the ones who perceive their need of forgiveness and salvation and act upon it. Compare Luke 7:36-50.

GOALS
1. To grow in appreciation of Jesus' great power to deliver and strengthen those who trust in him.

GREEN LEAF BIBLE SERIES

    2. To grow in understanding of the grace of God: that God mightily desires people to believe in him. The corollary is that unbelief results from human hardness and fickleness.

    3. To understand that Jesus was assisted in his ministry by a considerable number of people

DISCUSSION QUESTIONS
1. What is the point of Jesus' comment contrasting his ministry with that of John the Baptist (Luke 7:18-23)?

2. What was there about the faith of the centurion that made Jesus especially marvel (Luke 7:1-10)?

3. What is the key to understanding the parable of the sower?

4. Why did Jesus make the statement regarding his mother and his brothers in Luke 8:21?

PROJECTS
1. Display pictures that illustrate various parts of the parable of the sower (Luke 8:4-15).

2. Have students act out Jesus' encounter with the centurion (Luke 7:1-10) or the raising of the son of the widow of Nain (Luke 7:11-17).

3. Make a list of those times that people were raised from the dead in the gospels.

Luke

Teacher's Outline

THE GOSPEL OF LUKE

LESSON #7, JESUS AS THE DIVINE SON

PASSAGE TO STUDY: Luke 9:10b-62

SUGGESTIONS FOR SCRIPTURE TO BE READ IN CLASS

Basic	Supplementary	The feeding of 5000
Luke 9:10-17	Matthew 16:13-28	Matthew 14:13-21
Luke 9:18-22	Matthew 17:1-8	Mark 6:30-44
Luke 9:23-27	II Peter 1:16-18	Luke 9:10-17
Luke 9:57-62	I John 1:1-4	John 6:1-14

MEMORY VERSE FOR JANUARY
Luke 9:23, "If any man would come after me, let him deny himself and take up his cross daily and follow me."

BASIC CONCEPTS
1. The formal recognition by Peter (on behalf of the disciples) that Jesus was the Messiah (Luke 9:20)

2. The confirmation of Jesus as Messiah by other events recorded in this part of the gospel
    a. the feeding of a large multitude (Luke 9:10-17)
    b. the transfiguration experience (Luke 9:28-30)
    c. the healing of the boy who was possessed by a demon (Luke 9:37-43)

3. The authority of Jesus as Messiah in commanding those who believe in him to be his fully committed followers:
    a. Luke 9:23-26
    b. Luke 9:57-62

GOALS
1. To understand the extensiveness of the claims that Jesus makes on those who believe in him, and the foundation of those claims in his divine appointment and authority.

2. To understand more of the nature of Jesus Christ as revealed in the transfiguration:
    a. his God-nature seen more clearly in this manifestation of his glory (Luke 9:29)
    b. his eternity seen in his conversation with Moses and Elijah (Luke 9:30,31)

GREEN LEAF BIBLE SERIES

      c. the recognition by God the Father of <u>his uniqueness and superiority</u> (Luke 9:34,35)

3. To view something of the humanity and weakness of the disciples, and thereby more fully comprehend the doctrine of salvation by grace
   a. Luke 9:12,13
   b. Luke 9:33
   c. Luke 9:40,41
   d. Luke 9:46-48
   e. Luke 9:49,50
   f. Luke 9:53-55

DISCUSSION QUESTIONS
1. What did Jesus mean when he said that those who come after him should take up their crosses daily?

2. What do you think was the main purpose of the transfiguration experience?

3. Why does Jesus make the kinds of demands upon people that we read of in this section? See especially Luke 9:23-26 and 57-62.

PROJECTS
1. Do a flannelgraph or draw pictures of the transfiguration.

2. Have the students act out Luke 9:46-48.

3. Record a journal entry for Peter, James, or John describing their experiences and emotions at the transfiguration.

Luke

Teacher's Outline

THE GOSPEL OF LUKE

LESSON #8, JESUS' COMMISSIONINGS OF HIS DISCIPLES TO WITNESS

PASSAGES TO STUDY: Luke 9:1-10a; 10:1-24; 24:44-53

SUGGESTIONS FOR SCRIPTURE TO BE READ IN CLASS

Basic	Supplementary
Luke 9:1-9	Matthew 28:19,20
Luke 10:1-12	John 4:35-38
Luke 10:13-24	Acts 1:6-8
Luke 24:44-53	

MEMORY VERSE FOR JANUARY
Luke 9:23, "If any man would come after me, let him deny himself and take up his cross daily and follow me."

BASIC CONCEPTS
1. That the followers of Jesus Christ are commissioned to bear witness and testimony on his behalf. The repeated emphasis Jesus gives to witness indicates that it is to be of central importance.

2. God enables those whom he calls:
   a. Luke 9:1. He gave them power and authority.
   b. Luke 10:17-19. He gave them authority over all the power of the enemy--so that nothing would hurt them.
   c. Luke 24:49. They were to be clothed with power from on high.

3. Christian witness is to be offered--but not forced.
   a. Luke 9:5
   b. Luke 10:10,11

4. Of the $4\frac{1}{2}$ billion people in the world, about 1.2 billion are identified as Christians.

GOALS
1. To help pupils understand that the commands of Jesus apply to them as much as to others

2. To understand that when God calls a person to do something, he will also supply that person's needs and give sufficient strength

GREEN LEAF BIBLE SERIES

    3. To help people more fully realize that there are more people to be ministered to and to be won to Christ today than at any other time in history

DISCUSSION QUESTIONS
1. What are some principles of Christian witness that we learn of in Luke 9:1-6?

2. How does Jesus' statement in Luke 10:2 apply to us?

3. How should we respond to Jesus' statement in Luke 10:16?

4. If someone said, "what difference does it make whether a Christian is a witness?", how would you respond?

PROJECTS
1. List some of the resources that God gives to those who are witnesses for him.

2. Have pupils list several ways that they can fulfill Jesus' commission to be witnesses.

Luke

Teacher's Outline

THE GOSPEL OF LUKE

LESSON #9, A TRUE RELATIONSHIP TO GOD

PASSAGE TO STUDY: Luke 10:25-11:52

SUGGESTIONS FOR SCRIPTURE TO BE READ IN CLASS
Basic	Supplementary
Luke 10:25-37	Genesis 4:9
Luke 11:1-13	Leviticus 19:18
Luke 11:37-52	Isaiah 61:1,2

MEMORY VERSE FOR FEBRUARY
John 16:24, "Hitherto you have asked nothing in my name; ask, and you will receive, that your joy may be full."

BASIC CONCEPTS
1. Love for our neighbors, which manifests itself in being involved in their needs (Luke 10:25-37), is of great importance.

2. God desires for those who believe in him to pray, and he will graciously respond to their prayers (Luke 11:1-13).

3. One of the explanations of the power and dynamism of Jesus' ministry by his enemies was that he exercised evil powers. Jesus, however, clearly refuted such reasoning.
   a. Luke 11:14-23
   b. John 8:48-52

4. Some biblical truths have higher priority than others (Luke 11:42).

GOALS
1. To better understand the two great commandments (Luke 10:27) through the teachings and incidents related in this section:
   a. the parable of the good Samaritan (Luke 10:29-37) as an illustration of who one's neighbor is
   b. prayer as an exercise in loving God (11:1-13)
   c. misinterpreting Jesus' mission and motives as the opposite of love for God (Luke 11:14-23)
   d. taking care of secondary matters and neglecting the things that are of most importance to God
      1) Luke 10:38-42
      2) Luke 11:37-52

GREEN LEAF BIBLE SERIES

    2. To better understand the importance of obedience (doing things God's way):
       a. Luke 10:38-42
       b. Luke 11:23
       c. Luke 11:28
       d. Luke 11:42

DISCUSSION QUESTIONS
1. What is the answer to the lawyer's question, "And who is my neighbor?" Luke 10:29)?

2. What was Martha's problem (Luke 10:38-42)?

3. What did Jesus mean by the statement, "Your eye is the lamp of your body;" (Luke 11:34)?

4. Did Jesus condemn tithing when speaking to the Pharisees (Luke 11:42)?

PROJECTS
1. Act out the parable of the good Samaritan (Luke 10:29-37), or have the students tell the story from the viewpoint of each of the persons in the parable.

2. Discuss if there are any "neighbors" that we tend to pass by in our day.

3. Discuss what prayer is, times and places for prayer, and what the Lord's Prayer means phrase by phrase on the student's level. Discuss answers to prayers that may seem not to be answered.

Luke

Teacher's Outline

THE GOSPEL OF LUKE

LESSON #10, KEYS TO DISCIPLESHIP I

PASSAGE TO STUDY: Luke 11:53-13:30

SUGGESTIONS FOR SCRIPTURE TO BE READ IN CLASS
  Basic
  Luke 12:4-12
  Luke 12:13-21
  Luke 12:32-40
  Luke 13:10-17
  Luke 13:22-35

MEMORY VERSE FOR FEBRUARY
  John 16:24, "Hitherto you have asked nothing in my name; ask, and you will receive, that your joy may be full."

BASIC CONCEPTS
  1. We are accountable before God for everything that we say and do.
     a. Luke 12:2,3
     b. Luke 13:6-9
     c. Matthew 5:22,23

  2. It is of utmost importance to confess Christ as Savior and to follow him.
     a. Luke 12:4,5
     b. Luke 12:8,9
     c. Luke 13:1-5
     d. Luke 13:23-30

  3. A desire for the things of this world may blind a person to his spiritual needs.
     a. Luke 12:13-21

  4. We can trust God to supply our material needs when we give priority to his kingdom.
     a. Luke 12:22-31
     b. Luke 12:33,34

  5. The follower of Jesus Christ is to be ready for his return.
     a. Luke 12:20
     b. Luke 12:35-40
     c. Luke 12:42-48

GREEN LEAF BIBLE SERIES

    6. The kingdom of God is going to grow and triumph.
       a. Luke 12:32
       b. Luke 13:18-21

GOALS
1. To be able to state the basic concepts of this section in one's own words

2. That each person will choose to give Christ and his kingdom highest priority in his life

3. To understand that many popular and widely accepted concepts are fallacious, and will lead to spiritual destruction

DISCUSSION QUESTIONS
1. How do we acknowledge Jesus before men (Luke 12:8,9)?

2. What was the rich farmer's problem?

3. Why does Jesus warn against anxiety?

4. How can anxiety be avoided?

PROJECTS
1. List those occasions that Luke notes large crowds hearing or following Jesus.

2. Act out Luke 12:35-40.

3. Prepare a poster with the weather signs of Luke 12:54-56 and with parallel signs of the times for the present day.

4. Draw a picture illustrating Luke 13:22-30.

Luke

Teacher's Outline

THE GOSPEL OF LUKE

LESSON #11, KEYS TO DISCIPLESHIP II

PASSAGE: Luke 13:32-14:35

SUGGESTIONS FOR SCRIPTURE TO BE READ IN CLASS
  Basic
  Luke 14:1-14
  Luke 14:15-24
  Luke 14:25-35

MEMORY VERSE FOR FEBRUARY
  John 16:24, "Hitherto you have asked nothing in my name; ask, and you will receive, that your joy may be full."

BASIC CONCEPTS
  1. God has a continuing program for the nation of Israel. See Luke 13:34,35.

  2. Humility is an essential quality of the followers of Jesus Christ. See Luke 14:7-11.

  3. Christian love and discipleship are expressed in doing good and being kind to those who cannot repay us. See Luke 14:12-14.

  4. Many fail to respond to the opportunity of participating in the kingdom of God. See Luke 14:15-24.

  5. Many who seem to be unlikely candidates will be welcomed into the kingdom of God. See Luke 14:12-14.

  6. The disciple of Jesus Christ must be willing to put everything else aside in order to follow Jesus (Luke 14:25-35). Please compare Concept 3 in Lesson #7 and Concept 2 in Lesson #10, which are closely related.

GOALS
  1. Review: To be able to identify all of the significant people in the gospel of Luke to this point:
     Herod, King of Judea   Zechariah
     Elizabeth   Mary
     Joseph   Anna
     Simeon   John the Baptist

85

GREEN LEAF BIBLE SERIES

    Gabriel   Caesar Augustus
    Herod, tetrarch of Galilee Simon (Peter)
    James   John
    Levi (Matthew)   Martha
    Mary

2. To comprehend the unifying theme of this section of Luke (10:25-14:35): the centrality of Jesus Christ; the absolute importance of giving him first place in one's life.

DISCUSSION QUESTIONS

1. In what way do people improperly exalt themselves?

2. What does it mean to humble oneself?

3. In reference to the great banquet, what kinds of excuses would people offer today?

4. What does Jesus mean when he refers to hating father and mother, etc.?

5. How does one count the cost of discipleship? See Luke 14:26-33.

PROJECT

1. Do a study of God's continuing purposes for the people of Israel or with a few drawings or symbols illustrate what the Bible has to say about Israel:
   a. Abraham-Isaac-Jacob
   b. twelve families--Egypt
   c. slavery in Egypt/prayer to God for deliverance
   d. the Exodus
   e. the promised land
   f. a great nation
   g. division and decline
   h. conquest and captivity
   i. return and renewal
   j. continuing dispersion and suffering
   k. a new nation (1948)
   l. Israel becoming a part of the kingdom of God (Luke 13:35; Romans 11:24-29)
   m. the return of Jesus Christ

Luke

Teacher's Outline

THE GOSPEL OF LUKE

LESSON #12, THREE PARABLES ON THE LOVE OF GOD

PASSAGE TO STUDY: Luke 15:1-32

SUGGESTIONS FOR SCRIPTURE TO BE READ IN CLASS
   Basic
   Luke 15:1-7
   Luke 15:8-10
   Luke 15:11-24

MEMORY VERSE FOR FEBRUARY
   John 16:24, "Hitherto you have asked nothing in my name; ask, and you will receive, that your joy may be full."

BASIC CONCEPTS
   1. God's love extends to the unlikely and the unlovely
      a. Romans 5:6-11; especially Romans 5:8, "But God shows his love for us in that while we were yet sinners Christ died for us."
      b. I Timothy 1:13-16; especially I Timothy 1:15, "The saying is sure and worthy of full acceptance, that Christ Jesus came into the world to save sinners..."
      c. Luke 5:28-32; especially Luke 5:32, "I have not come to call the righteous, but sinners to repentance."

   2. God's love is a seeking love. We are saved on his initiative.
      a. John 3:16
      b. Titus 3:4-7
      c. Ephesians 1:3-6
      d. Acts 9:1-9

   3. Repentance is one of the basic keys to a right relationship with God.
      a. Luke 15:17-19; especially Luke 15:8, "I will arise and go to my father and I will say to him, "Father, I have sinned against heaven and before you;"
      b. Mark 1:14,15, "Now after John was arrested, Jesus came into Galilee, preaching the gospel of God, and saying, 'The time is fulfilled, and the kingdom of God is at hand; repent, and believe in the gospel.'"
      c. Luke 13:1-5
      d. Luke 17:3,4

GREEN LEAF BIBLE SERIES

      e. Luke 19:1-10; especially 19:8, "And Zacchaeus stood and said to the Lord, 'Behold, Lord, the half of my goods I give to the poor; and if I have defrauded any one of anything, I restore it fourfold.'"

4. God receives and accepts those who come to him.
   a. Luke 15:22-24
   b. John 6:37, "All that the Father gives me will come to me, and him who comes to me I will not cast out."
   c. Acts 2:21, "And it shall be that whoever calls upon the name of the Lord shall be saved."
   d. I John 5:1, "Every one who believes that Jesus is the Christ is a child of God,..."

GOALS
1. To enable each student to relate these three parables in his or her own words

2. To enable each student to state how these parables are descriptive of his or her relationship to God

DISCUSSION QUESTIONS
1. What teaching do the three parables have in common?

2. Why did the young man want to leave home?

3. Who or what does the elder son represent?

PROJECTS
1. Act out the drama of the lost coin (Luke 15:8-10).

2. Introduce the parables by discussing reactions to situations in the students' lives, such as finding a lost pet, a lost toy, or a present day runaway returning home.

3. Have students choose one of the following topics for a newspaper article:
   a. Shepherd Finds Lost Sheep
   b. Woman Finds Silver Coin
   c. Son Returns Home
   d. Have an editorial column entitled "Angels Rejoice Over Repentant Sinners"

Luke

Teacher's Outline

THE GOSPEL OF LUKE

LESSON #13, TEACHINGS ON COMMITMENT

PASSAGE TO STUDY: Luke 16:1-17:19

SUGGESTIONS FOR SCRIPTURE TO BE READ IN CLASS
Basic	Supplementary
Luke 16:1-9	Matthew 11:13
Luke 16:19-31	John 1:17
Luke 17:1-10	Hebrews 9:15
Luke 17:22-37	
Luke 17:11-19 (could be used in lower grades.)	

MEMORY VERSE FOR MARCH
  James 3:17, "But the wisdom from above is first pure, then peaceable, gentle, open to reason, full of mercy and good fruits, without uncertainty or insincerity."

BASIC CONCEPTS
  1. Jesus commends the person who uses the things of this world to accomplish spiritual purposes.

  2. If what Jesus said about himself is true, he must have our full devotion and loyalty. Divided loyalty toward Jesus Christ is inappropriate and impossible.

  3. "You cannot serve God and mammon", is illustrated many places in the Bible:
     a. Achan--Joshua 7:16-26
     b. Gehazi, the servant of Elisha--II Kings 5:19b-27
     c. the rich farmer--Luke 12:13-21
     d. the rich young ruler--Matthew 19:16-22
     e. the rich man and Lazarus--Luke 16:19-31

  4. People have sufficient cause to believe in God, if they will believe (Luke 16:31).

  5. We are to praise God for his love and care for us.

GOAL
  1. To enable each person to explain the significance of the Parable of the steward (16:1-9) and of the rich man and Lazarus (16:19-31).

GREEN LEAF BIBLE SERIES

DISCUSSION QUESTIONS
1. What is the point of the parable of the unjust steward?

2. What did Jesus mean when he said that people enter the kingdom of God violently?

3. What does the parable of the rich man and Lazarus teach us about the state of those who are lost?

PROJECTS
1. Discuss the meaning of Luke 16:8, "...the sons of this world are wiser in their own generation than the sons of light."

2. Have everyone in the class draw a sketch depicting some aspect of the parable of the rich man and Lazarus.

3. Have students prepare scenes for an evangelistic scroll theater presentation from Luke 17:22-37 entitled "One Is Taken, One Is Left Behind" using such scenes as:
    a. some people mistakenly claiming that Jesus has come
    b. life in the days of Noah
    c. destruction by flood
    d. life in the days of Lot
    e. destruction of Sodom
    f. the days of the 20th century
    g. the coming of Christ (Luke 16:24)
    h. seeking to preserve life vs. losing it
    i. Jesus receiving his own unto himself

4. Study the various passages in the gospels that deal with the subject of divorce.

Luke

Teacher's Outline

THE GOSPEL OF LUKE

LESSON #14, TEACHINGS AND INCIDENTS ON THE WAY TO JERUSALEM

PASSAGE TO STUDY: Luke 17:20-19:27

SUGGESTIONS FOR SCRIPTURE TO BE READ IN CLASS
<u>Basic</u>
Luke 18:1-8
Luke 18:9-27
Luke 18:28-30
Luke 18:31-43
Luke 19:1-10

MEMORY VERSE FOR MARCH
James 3:17, "But the wisdom from above is first pure, then peaceable, gentle, open to reason, full of mercy and good fruits, without uncertainty or insincerity."

BASIC CONCEPTS
1. Christ will return at a time when he is not expected, but all will know it when he comes.

2. Failure to believe in Christ will result in exclusion from the kingdom of God.

3. God will speedily answer the prayers of those who faithfully continue in prayer to him. See Luke 18:7,8.

4. The persons who seek to serve rather than those who seek places of honor are the ones who will be exalted in the kingdom of God. See Luke 18:14,17.

5. It is difficult to turn away from the possessions and pleasures of this life, but those who do so for the sake of the kingdom of God will receive abundant blessings both in this life and the life to come.
   a. Luke 18:25
   b. Luke 18:29,30
   c. Luke 19:1-10

6. Jesus Christ graciously receives those who come to him.

GREEN LEAF BIBLE SERIES

7. God expects us to make good use of the abilities and opportunities that he has given to us. Those who do so will be given greater opportunity.

8. Jesus was aware of his crucifixion ahead of time and sought to prepare the disciples for that event. See Luke 18:31-34.

GOALS
1. To comprehend certain principles regarding the return of Christ
   a. that it will be unexpected by the unbelieving community
   b. that it will be known to all when it occurs
   c. that absolute loyalty to Christ is vital in view of his return
   d. the consequences of unbelief

2. To locate the key verses that state or summarize the basic concepts of what Jesus was teaching

3. To be able to explain what it means to, "receive the kingdom of God like a child" (Luke 18:17)

DISCUSSION QUESTIONS
1. How will people know when Christ returns?

2. What is an improper attitude regarding the return of Christ?

3. What is the difference between persistence in prayer (Luke 18:1-18) and undue repetition in prayer (Matthew 6:7,8)?

4. Why did Jesus respond to the ruler (Luke 18:18-25) the way that he did?

PROJECTS
1. Act out the parable of the pounds (Luke 19:11-27).

2. Discuss the meaning of the parable of the widow and the unrighteous judge (Luke 18:1-8) and of the Pharisee and the tax collector (Luke 18:9-14).

3. Prepare a worksheet on prayer including biblical references which will help the students know how to pray, for which things to pray, and what the students will pray about.

4. Discuss tithing in connection with the parable of the rich young ruler and the example of Zacchaeus. Make mathematical computations based upon students' actual experiences. Discuss the 90% which is left.

Luke

Teacher's Outline

THE GOSPEL OF LUKE

LESSON #15, TRIUMPHAL ENTRY AND FINAL DISCOURSES

PASSAGE TO STUDY: Luke 19:28-21:38

SUGGESTIONS FOR SCRIPTURE TO BE READ IN CLASS
  Basic
  Luke 19:28-40
  Luke 19:41-48
  Luke 20:1-8
  Luke 20:19-26
  Luke 20:27-40
  Luke 21:1-9

MEMORY VERSE FOR MARCH
  James 3:17, "But the wisdom from above is first pure, then peaceable, gentle, open to reason, full of mercy and good fruits, without uncertainty or insincerity."

BASIC CONCEPTS
  1. Jesus Christ is the Messiah, worthy of all acclaim and reverence. He is the rightful ruler of Israel and of the whole earth.

  2. A true belief in the Messiah would bring deliverance from many calamities (Luke 19:41-44).

  3. On many occasions Jesus spoke clearly, ahead of time, of the suffering and crucifixion that faced him.

  4. Jesus responded so well to the questions that were asked of him that his enemies became unwilling to put any more questions to him.

  5. The principle of sacrifice is one of the biblical standards of giving. It is not the amount that a person gives, but the sacrifice that is made in giving the gift that is highly regarded by God.

  6. Great difficulties and calamities are to come upon the world. They are not to cause fear and dismay in the one who believes in Christ; rather they are to be signs of encouragement that the return of Christ and his redemption is near.

GREEN LEAF BIBLE SERIES

GOALS
1. To understand that the relationship of people with God has an important effect upon their happiness and the functioning of society.

2. To understand that the Palm Sunday welcome of Jesus into Jerusalem was a clear recognition by many that he was the Messiah.

3. To understand that salvation in Jesus Christ is greatly to be desired in spite of difficulties that may be encountered by those who commit themselves to him.

DISCUSSION QUESTIONS
1. Why did Jesus respond the way he did to the question regarding his authority (Luke 20:2)?

2. What purpose was served by Jesus' triumphal (Palm Sunday) entrance into Jerusalem?

3. Who is Jesus talking about when he refers to the tenants of the vineyard (Luke 20:9-16)?

4. What are some basic principles taught in this section regarding the return of Christ?

PROJECTS
1. Display a map of Jerusalem that indicates the gates of the city and the surrounding area. Use pictures or markers to indicate Jesus' entrance into the city.

2. Draw a picture that indicates some of the things that Luke 21:10-36 conveys to you. This could be in the form of a mural or posters entitled "The Kingdom of God is at Hand."

3. Prepare a play to be given at a neighborhood Easter party or at a convalescent home. Suggested topics are "The Entry Into Jerusalem" or "Events at the Temple."

4. Have students prepare a cartoon strip for the parable of the vineyard (Luke 20:9-16).

5. Begin thinking of a way for the class to share the joy of Easter with someone else.

6. From all of the gospels make a list of the times that the leaders of the Jews threatened Jesus' life and/or plotted against him.

Luke

Teacher's Outline

THE GOSPEL OF LUKE

LESSON #16, FINAL EVENTS/ARREST AND TRIAL/RESURRECTION AND CONSUMMATION

PASSAGE TO STUDY: Luke 22:1-24:43

SUGGESTIONS FOR SCRIPTURE TO BE READ IN CLASS

Basic	Supplementary
Luke 22:1-13	Matthew 26:14-28:20
Luke 22:14-23	Mark 14:10-16:8
Luke 22:39-46	John 13:1-21:25
Luke 22:47-53	
Luke 23:1-12	
Luke 23:13-24	
Luke 23:44-56	
Luke 24:1-11	

MEMORY VERSE FOR MARCH
James 3:17, "But the wisdom from above is first pure, then peaceable, gentle, open to reason, full of mercy and good fruits, without uncertainty or insincerity."

BASIC CONCEPTS
1. The immediate cause of Jesus' death was the plotting of the leaders of the Jews, the betrayal of Judas, and the perfidy of Pilate.

2. Jesus confidently looked forward to his triumph over death and the establishment of his kingdom.
    a. Luke 22:18
    b. Luke 22:28-30
    c. Luke 22:69

3. Prayer is one of the main defenses of the Christian against temptation.
    a. Luke 22:32
    b. Luke 22:40
    c. Luke 22:46

4. Jesus was publicly crucified and died. Multitudes witnessed this event, and knowledge of it was widespread.
    a. Matthew 27:50
    b. Matthew 27:55-61

GREEN LEAF BIBLE SERIES

      c. Mark 15:37-47
      d. Luke 27:17,18
      e. John 19:30-42

5. The resurrection of Jesus Christ is well attested:
   a. the circumstances at the tomb on the first day of the week were consistent with his resurrection
   b. angels testified to his resurrection (Luke 24:4-7)
   c. his death and resurrection were clearly foretold in the Old Testament
      1) Psalm 22, especially verses 1, 7, 8, 14-18
      2) Isaiah 52:13-53:21
      3) Psalm 16:9,20 (compare Acts 13:32-35)
      4) Psalm 69:19-21
   d. many saw Jesus following his resurrection (I Corinthians 15:5-8)

6. Jesus' resurrection was not just the continued existence of his spirit. He was raised bodily from the dead. The tomb was empty (Luke 24:36-43).

GOALS
1. To understand the meaning and the practices of the Passover. See Exodus chapter 12.

2. To better understand the impending sacrifice which Christ would make and to connect it with the Passover. See Isaiah 53:7, I Corinthians 5:7, John 1:29, and I Peter 1:19.

3. To better understand the significance of the Lord's Supper. See Jeremiah 31:31-34, Hebrews chapter 10, and I Corinthians 11:23-28.

4. To comprehend and be able to relate the sequence of the events in the garden, at the high priest's house and before Pilate and Herod

5. To be able to relate the four basic areas of substantiation for the resurrection

6. To be able to name the people involved in the resurrection account in Luke

DISCUSSION QUESTIONS
1. Why did Judas betray Jesus?

2. What motivated Pilate to do the things that he did?

Luke

3. How do you think the disciples felt after Jesus' arrest, trial, and crucifixion?

4. What brought about a change in the disciples?

PROJECTS
1. Listen to portions of Handel's <u>Messiah</u>.

2. Sample the unleavened Jewish bread, matzo.

3. Act out the preparation for the Passover.

4. Discuss the significance of Communion for the students and how it is observed in this particular church.

5. Do a mural covering the events after the Last Supper in the upper room.

6. Have students relate in their own words or with illustrations the sequence of events concerning Jesus, beginning with his arrest.

7. Read as a play the passages with a large amount of dialogue.

GREEN LEAF BIBLE SERIES

Teacher's Outline

THE COSPEL OF LUKE

LESSON #17, QUIZ

1. What are the names of the father and mother of John the Baptist?

    a. _____ b. _____

2. What was the name of the ruler of the Roman Empire when Jesus was born? _____

3. What happened to the father of John the Baptist from the time that the angel spoke to him until John was born? _____
_____

4. Name the two elderly people in the temple who blessed Jesus when he was brought for the rites of purification.

    a. _____ b. _____

5. What was Jesus' approximate age when he began his ministry? ____

6. What were the three temptations of Jesus after the forty days in the wilderness?

    a. _____
    b. _____
    c. _____

7. Name six of the twelve disciples.

    a. _____ d. _____
    b. _____ e. _____
    c. _____ f. _____

8. Where was Jesus born? _____

9. In what town did Jesus live most of his life? _____

Luke

10. What other book in the New Testament was written by Luke? _____

11. List eight cities or geographic areas visited by Jesus.

   a. _____ e. _____

   b. _____ f. _____

   c. _____ g. _____

   d. _____ h. _____

12. In the parable of the sower, what does the seed represent? _____

13. List four indications or evidences that Jesus was the Messiah.

   a. _____

   b. _____

   c. _____

   d. _____

14. What was Matthew's occupation before he began following Jesus?

   _____

15. What two shorter parables are associated with the parable of the prodigal son?

   a. _____ b. _____

16. Cite at least three passages from Luke that indicate that large crowds came to hear Jesus.

   a. _____ c. _____

   b. _____

17. What advice did Jesus give for those who are invited to a banquet and don't know where to sit? _____

GREEN LEAF BIBLE SERIES

18. What are two truths that we learn about the second coming of Christ from Luke?

   a. _____

   b. _____

19. Who climbed up into a sycamore tree to see Jesus? _____

    In what city did this man live? _____

20. Certain hard questions were put to Jesus during the last week of his ministry--with what did two of them have to do?

   a. _____

   b. _____

21. Who betrayed Jesus? _____

22. Who ordered Jesus to be crucified? _____

23. List three individuals or groups who were witnesses to the resurrection of Jesus according to the gospel of Luke.

   a. _____

   b. _____

   c. _____

HEROES OF THE BIBLE

Unit Three   The Book of Exodus
11 Weeks

GREEN LEAF BIBLE SERIES

YEAR ONE, UNIT THREE

THE BOOK OF EXODUS

Week One	INTRODUCTION/THE SITUATION OF THE ISRAELITES IN EGYPT/THE BIRTH OF MOSES	Exodus 1:1-2:22
Week Two	GOD'S CALL TO MOSES	Exodus 2:23-4:26
Week Three	MOSES AND AARON PETITION PHAROAH	Exodus 4:27-7:24
Week Four	THE PLAGUES UPON THE EGYPTIANS	Exodus 7:25-10:29
Week Five	THE PASSOVER	Exodus 11:1-13:16
Week Six	THE DELIVERANCE OF ISRAEL	Exodus 13:17-15:21
Week Seven	THE JOURNEY TO SINAI	Exodus 15:22-18:27
Week Eight	THE GIVING OF THE LAW AT SINAI	Exodus 19:1-24:11
Week Nine	GOD GIVES THE ISRAELITES A SYSTEM OF WORSHIP	Exodus 24:12-31:18
Week Ten	THE IDOLATRY OF THE ISRAELITES	Exodus 32:1-35:3
Week Eleven	THE CONSTRUCTION AND FURNISHING OF THE TABERNACLE	Exodus 35:4-40:38

REVIEW AND QUIZ (to be accomplished by combining with Lesson #11, combining two previous lessons, or extending the course one week)

Exodus

THE BOOK OF EXODUS

| CURRICULUM RESOURCE LIST | APPROXIMATE PRICE |

BOOKS

My Book of Bible Stories; Standard	6.95
Arch Books; Concordia	.79
"Simon Was Safe" (Exodus 7:19-12:42)	
"The Great Escape" (Exodus 3:1-15:1)	
"The Princess and the Baby" (Exodus 1:8-2:10)	
Bible Story Cartoons, Norman Lynch; Standard	
The Old Testament in 16 books (in case)	9.95
Book 5: "Moses in Egypt"	.59
Book 6: "Moses in the Wilderness"	.59
Mini Pop-Up Books; Standard	2.50
The Story of Moses	
Daily Study Bible: Exodus, H. L. Ellison; Westminster	5.95
A History of Israel, John Bright; Westminster	18.95
The Bible in Pictures for Little Eyes, Kenneth Taylor; Moody	9.95
Basic Bible Readers; Standard	4.95
Bible Adventures	
Bible Heroes	
Exodus, Today's English Version; American Bible Society	.59

MAPS, CHARTS, TIMELINES

Fun with Bible Geography: Teacher's Guide to the Holy Lands	3.75
Lands; Accent	
Bible Maps and Charts, No. 2 (Egypt to Canaan); Standard	3.95

TRANSPARENCIES, DUPLICATING MASTERS, FILMSTRIPS, FILMS

Tell Me A Story: Great Bible Stories #5, Cassette side 1	4.95
"A Brother Who Remembered" (Joseph); side 2 "A Baby in	
a Basket"; Augsberg	
Filmstrips; Concordia	5.75
"Moses, Called by God"	
"Moses, Leader of God's People"	
Records for above filmstrips	3.45
Jensen Bible Study Charts (transparencies); Moody	9.95
General Survey: Volume I	
Old Testament: Volume II	
Old Testament Puzzle Masters; Standard	5.95

FLANNELGRAPH, POSTERS, PICTURES

Old Testament Pictograph Stories; Standard	
Stories About Moses	4.50
The Tabernacle Pictograph; Standard	4.50

GREEN LEAF BIBLE SERIES

Suede-Graph: Baby Moses; Scripture Press	2.75
Coordinating cassette	4.25
Moses and the Burning Bush; Scripture Press	2.75

ACTIVITY BOOKS, PROJECTS, GAMES, PUZZLES

Book by Book Old Testament Quizzes; Victor Books	1.50
Moses: Journey to Freedom; American Bible Society	.35
Moses: Journey to a New Land; American Bible Society	.35
Tabernacle Model to Make; Standard	2.50
Miracles of the Old Testament; Standard	2.75
Bible Times Village to Make; Standard	2.50
Creative Bible Activities for Children; Victor Books	5.95
Bible Story Inlay Puzzles (Baby Moses); Standard	1.49
Frances Hook Inlay Puzzles; Standard	1.19
God Watches Over Baby Moses	
Old Testament Lotto; Standard	4.95

Exodus

THE BOOK OF EXODUS

The book of Exodus is a bridge between Genesis and the other books of the Old Testament. Genesis is a book of beginnings: the beginning of the world, the beginning of the human race, and the beginning of a covenant people. Exodus tells us how that covenant people, beginning as a small clan, became a nation of more than a million people. It tells us how an exceedingly favorable situation in Egypt deteriorated until the Israelites became slaves who were subject to arduous labor and whose lives could be extinguished at the whim of a Pharoah. It details the deliverance of God, so that by mighty wonders these people left Egypt and established themselves in the Sinai wilderness. There, as God's chosen people, they received the law and instructions regarding the system of worship whereby their relationship with God was to be regulated. At Sinai they were more definitely established as the people of God. The events related in Exodus probably take place in the fifteenth century B.C. (1400-1500 B.C.). However, the Egyptian dates for this period are not precisely determined. A variety of dates from 1200-1500 B.C. are offered by biblical scholars. The paramount human personality in the book is that of Moses, one of the most godly men of any age. His dynamic leadership at a crucial phase in the history of his people secured for him a major place in sacred history and a significant place in secular history. He is recognized by both Jews and Gentiles as one of the great men of all time.

OUTLINE OF EXODUS
   I.   THE ISRAELITES IN EGYPT (1:1-13:16)

       A. Introduction (1:1-22)
          1. The descendants of Jacob increase in Egypt (1:1-7)

          2. The Egyptians put the Israelites into slavery (1:8-14)

          3. The Hebrew midwives are commanded to kill all male babies, but they disobey (1:15-22)

       B. The first part of Moses' life (2:1-22)
          1. Moses' birth and his adoption by Pharoah's daughter (2:1-10)

          2. Abortive attempts by Moses to help his people (2:11-15a)

          3. Moses flees to the land of Midian (2:15b-22)

       C. God's call to Moses (2:23-4:26)
          1. God takes note of the difficult situation of the Israelites (2:23-25)

GREEN LEAF BIBLE SERIES

      2. God speaks to Moses out of the burning bush and commissions him to be the leader of his people (3:1-12)

      3. God gives Moses further instructions (3:13-22)

      4. Moses protests that he has no credentials, and God gives him three signs (4:1-9)

      5. Moses protests his lack of eloquence; God assures him that Aaron will be his spokesman (4:10-17)

      6. Moses makes preparations to return to Egypt (4:18-26)

  D. The first approach to Pharoah and its consequences (4:27-6:9)
      1. Aaron meets Moses in the wilderness, and they tell the people of God's concern for them (4:27-31)

      2. Moses and Aaron request Pharoah to release the people (5:1-3)

      3. The reactions to that request (5:4-6:9)
        a. Pharoah rejects their request and adds to the work of the Israelites (5:4-14)
        b. the foremen of the people of Israel protest their increased burdens (5:15-21)
        c. God assures Moses that he will fulfill his covenant originally given to Abraham, Isaac, and Jacob (5:22-6:9)

  E. Subsequent approaches to Pharoah (6:10-7:24)
      1. God commands Moses to tell Pharoah to let the people of Israel leave (6:10-13)

      2. Genealogy pertaining to Moses and Aaron (6:14-27)

      3. God warns Moses and Aaron that Pharoah will not heed them (6:28-7:7)

      4. The First Miracle: Aaron's rod becomes a serpent (7:8-13)

      5. The Second Miracle: the Nile turns to blood (7:14-24)

  F. The judgments of God upon Egypt (7:25-13:16)
      1. The First Plague: Frogs (7:25-8:15)

      2. The Second Plague: Gnats (8:16-19)

Exodus

      3. The Third Plague: Flies (8:20-32)

      4. The Fourth Plague: Pestilence upon the cattle (9:1-7)

      5. The Fifth Plague: Boils (9:8-12)

      6. The Sixth Plague: Hail (9:13-35)

      7. The Seventh Plague: Locusts (10:3-20)

      8. The Eighth Plague: Darkness (10:21-29)

      9. A Final Plague to come (11:1-10)

     10. The Passover (12:1-51)

     11. A day of remembrance (13:1-16)

II. THE EXODUS (13:17-18:27)

    A. The deliverance of the people (13:17-15:21)
      1. The people move into the wilderness led by the pillar of cloud and the pillar of fire (13:17-22)

      2. The crossing of the Red Sea; the Egyptian Army is destroyed (14:1-31)

      3. The song of victory (15:1-21)

    B. Journey to Sinai (15:22-18:27)
      1. The Lord provides water (15:22-27)

      2. The provision of manna (16:1-36)

      3. God again provides water (17:1-7)

      4. Victory over Amalek (17:8-16)

      5. Moses welcomes his father-in-law (18:1-12)

      6. Judicial procedures established (18:13-27)

III. THE PEOPLE ARRIVE AT SINAI (19:1-40:38) (see also Numbers 10:10)

    A. The giving of the law at Sinai (19:1-24:11)
      1. God's covenant with the people (19:1-9a)

      2. God descends upon the mountain (19:9b-25)

GREEN LEAF BIBLE SERIES

       3. The Ten Commandments (20:1-17)

       4. General rules regarding worship (20:18-26)

       5. Civil law (21:1-23:11)

       6. Laws regarding worship (23:12-19)

       7. God promises to bless his people if they are faithful to him (23:20-33)

       8. The book of the covenant (24:1-8)

       9. The Lord reveals himself to Moses, Aaron, Nadab, Abihu, and seventy elders (24:9-11)

  B. The plan for the Tabernacle (24:12-31:18)
       1. Moses goes up on the mountain of God (24:12-18)

       2. Directions for making the tabernacle and its furnishings (25:1-27:21)

       3. The appointment of the priests and their apparel (28:1-43)

       4. The ordination of the priests (29:1-46)

       5. The incense altar (30:1-10)

       6. The half-shekel offering (30:11-16)

       7. The laver of bronze (30:17-21)

       8. The directions for the sacred anointing oil and incense (30:22-28)

       9. Ornamental work and keeping the Sabbath (31:1-18)

  C. The idolatry of the Israelites: their repentance and renewal (32:1-35:3)
       1. The golden calf (32:1-35)

       2. God condemns the people but assures Moses of his continuing presence (33:1-23)

       3. God makes a covenant with the people, and new tables of stone are made (34:1-28)

Exodus

      4. Moses returns to the people with the two tables; his face shines (34:29-35)

      5. The keeping of the Sabbath (35:1-3)

D. Provisions for and construction of the tabernacle and its furnishings (35:4-40:38)
    1. Preliminary (35:4-36:7)
      a. an offering is called for (35:4-9)
      b. the men are called to the work (35:10-19)
      c. the offering is received (35:20-29)
      d. Bezalel and Oholiab head up the work (35:30-36:7)

    2. The construction of the tabernacle and furnishings (36:8-38:20)
      a. the curtains (36:8-19)
      b. the frames (36:20-34)
      c. the veil, pillars, and screen (36:35-38)
      d. the ark (37:1-9)
      e. the table and its vessels (37:10-16)
      f. the lampstand (37:17-24)
      g. the altar of incense (37:25-28)
      h. the anointing oil (37:29)
      i. the altar of burnt offering (38:1-7)
      j. the laver (38:8)
      k. the court (38:9-20)

    3. A summary of the construction (38:21-31)
      a. garments for the priests (39:1-31)
      b. the completed work is brought to Moses (39:32-43)
      c. the tabernacle is erected and anointed by Moses (40:1-33)

E. The cloud covers the tent and the glory of the Lord fills the tabernacle (40:34-38)

GREEN LEAF BIBLE SERIES

Teacher's Outline

THE BOOK OF EXODUS

LESSON #1, INTRODUCTION/THE SITUATION OF THE ISRAELITES IN EGYPT/THE BIRTH OF MOSES

PASSAGE TO STUDY: Exodus 1:1-2:22

SUGGESTIONS FOR SCRIPTURE TO BE READ IN CLASS
  Basic   Supplementary
  Exodus 1:1-14   Hebrews 11:23-28
  Exodus 1:15-22   Acts 7:17-29
  Exodus 2:1-10
  Exodus 2:11-22

SCRIPTURE MEMORY FOR APRIL
  Titus 3:5, "he saved us, not because of deeds done by us in righteousness, but in virtue of his own mercy, by the washing of regeneration and renewal in the Holy Spirit,"

BASIC CONCEPTS
  1. The people of Israel became a large nation in Egypt.
     a. Exodus 1:7
     b. Exodus 1:9,10
     c. Exodus 1:12
     d. Exodus 1:20

  2. Moses' first attempt at leadership was a failure (Exodus 2:11-15).

  3. Egypt enjoyed the highest level of civilization in the world during the middle and second millenium B.C.

GOALS
  1. To understand the continuity of the people of Israel from Abraham, Isaac, and Jacob to the time of Moses

  2. To understand that the historical circumstances of the people of Israel in Egypt during the time of Moses would be used by God to fulfill his overall purpose of redemption

  3. To appreciate the background of Moses--out of which his call to leadership came

  4. To understand some of the reasons for the Egyptians' change in attitude toward the people of Israel:

Exodus

      a. growth in numbers
      b. material success
      c. separate tribal government
      d. possible changes in Egyptian government (from Dynasty XII through Hyksos' rule to succeeding dynasties)

DISCUSSION QUESTIONS
1. Why did the Egyptians change their attitude toward the people of Israel?

2. What do you think was in Moses' mind when he killed the Egyptian?

3. What do you think was in Moses' mind when he came to the land of Midian?

PROJECTS
1. Display pictures of Egypt as it was thought to look from 1900 to 1300 B.C.

2. Draw pictures or cartoons to illustrate major events in Moses' early life (his birth, killing the Egyptian, fleeing, working as a shepherd, etc.).

GREEN LEAF BIBLE SERIES

Teacher's Outline

THE BOOK OF EXODUS

LESSON #2, GOD'S CALL TO MOSES

PASSAGE TO STUDY: Exodus 2:23-4:26

SUGGESTIONS FOR SCRIPTURE TO BE READ IN CLASS

Basic	Supplementary
Exodus 2:23-3:12	Luke 20:37-40
Exodus 4:1-9	John 8:58
Exodus 4:10-17	Acts 7:30-44
Exodus 4:18-26	Psalm 103:7

SCRIPTURE MEMORY FOR APRIL
Titus 3:5, "he saved us, not because of deeds done by us in righteousness, but in virtue of his own mercy, by the washing of regeneration and renewal in the Holy Spirit,"

BASIC CONCEPTS
1. God has compassion on those who trust in him, and he will come to the aid of those who call upon him.

2. God needs human instruments to carry out his purposes.

3. God will equip and enable those whom he calls.

4. God wants to strengthen the faith of those who are inclined to believe in him. He will provide means for faith to grow.

GOALS
1. To be able to identify:
   a. Moses
   b. Aaron
   c. Midian
   d. Reuel/Jethro
   e. Horeb
   f. Zipporah
   g. Gershom

2. To be able to relate God's calling of Moses to God's previous dealings with Abraham, Isaac, and Jacob

3. To be able to name the three signs that God gave to Moses (Exodus 4:1-9):
   a. the rod turned to a serpent
   b. Moses' hand becoming leprous
   c. the water of the Nile River becoming blood

Exodus

DISCUSSION QUESTIONS
1. What was the occasion of God's intervening to help the people of Israel in Egypt?

2. Why did God call Moses to be involved in this purpose of delivering the people of Israel? Was he well qualified? Why not someone else?

3. What were some of Moses' objections to this assignment that God gave him?

4. What provisions did God make for Moses?

PROJECTS
1. Have the class discuss times when God has called them to do something and how he has helped them in doing it.

2. Trace Moses' journeys to and from Egypt on a map.

GREEN LEAF BIBLE SERIES

Teacher's Outline

THE BOOK OF EXODUS

LESSON #3, MOSES AND AARON PETITION PHAROAH

PASSAGE TO STUDY: Exodus 4:27-7:24

SUGGESTIONS FOR SCRIPTURE TO BE READ IN CLASS
Basic	Supplementary
Exodus 4:27-31	Exodus 6:2-13
Exodus 5:1-9	Exodus 7:1-7
Exodus 5:15-6:1	Exodus 7:8-13

SCRIPTURE MEMORY FOR APRIL
Titus 3:5, "he saved us, not because of deeds done by us in righteousness, but in virtue of his own mercy, by the washing of regeneration and renewal in the Holy Spirit,"

BASIC CONCEPTS
1. The initial response of the people of Israel was to welcome the leadership of Moses and Aaron. See Exodus 4:30,31.

2. Subsequently the people of Israel questioned that leadership.
   a. Exodus 5:20,21
   b. Exodus 6:9
   c. Exodus 6:12

3. God's undertaking to deliver the people of Israel was in response to his covenant established with Abraham, Isaac, and Jacob.
   a. Exodus 6:2-5
   b. Exodus 6:6-8

4. Moses protested his sin and, therefore, his inadequacy to the Lord. See Exodus 6:12 and 6:30.

5. The work of God and deliverance of the people of Israel was made possible by the obedience of Moses and Aaron. Compare Exodus 7:6.

6. The Pharoah of Joseph's time had acknowledged God and, indeed, sought his blessings. Joseph and his people were a witness to the Egyptians. By the time of Moses and Aaron (almost 400 years later) that witness had been thoroughly rejected. The hearts of the leaders of Egypt were completely closed to God. Compare Exodus 5:2.

Exodus

7. The obstinancy of Pharoah made necessary increasing displays of the power of God. See Exodus 7:3.

GOALS
1. To understand the ambivalent attitude of the people of Israel toward Moses and Aaron due to their weak faith in God

2. To appreciate the firm intent of God to fulfill his covenant with Abraham, Isaac, and Jacob

DISCUSSION QUESTIONS
1. Why did Pharoah refuse the requests of Moses and Aaron?

2. How did God respond to the doubts of the people of Israel? See especially Exodus 5:22-6:9.

3. What are some things that we learn about God in this section?

PROJECTS
1. From resource books, prepare a list of the gods of the Egyptians.

2. Collect pictures from the National Geographic and other resources of scenes of Egypt and Egyptian life that would relate to the period 1600-1300 B.C.

3. Discuss our ambivalent attitudes toward God, and how such attitudes manifest themselves in our everyday lives.

4. Read and discuss Romans 9:14-24 and Romans 1:18-28 in connection with the hardening of Pharoah's heart.

5. Make a list of the promises of God that Moses was to relate to the Israelites from Exodus 6:6-8.

GREEN LEAF BIBLE SERIES

Teacher's Outline

THE BOOK OF EXODUS

LESSON #4, THE PLAGUES UPON THE EGYPTIANS

PASSAGE TO STUDY: Exodus 7:25-10:29

SUGGESTIONS FOR SCRIPTURE TO BE READ IN CLASS

Basic	Supplementary
Exodus 7:25-8:15	Psalm 105:26-45
Exodus 8:16-19	
Exodus 9:13-21	
Exodus 9:22-35	
Exodus 10:1-11	
Exodus 10:21-29	

SCRIPTURE MEMORY FOR APRIL
   Titus 3:5, "he saved us, not because of deeds done by us in righteousness, but in virtue of his own mercy, by the washing of regeneration and renewal in the Holy Spirit,"

BASIC CONCEPTS
1. The consistency of God: he keeps his promises. In spite of Moses' reluctance and the people's reluctance and in spite of stubborn opposition of Pharoah and the Egyptians, God performs his covenant with Abraham, Isaac, and Jacob by delivering the people of Israel from Egypt.

2. The grace of God: though the Egyptians are worthy of the judgment of God, he seeks to spare them so that by the signs given through Moses and Aaron they might believe the word of God. The plagues are progressively more severe so that, perhaps, Pharoah and the Egyptians may obey before the most severe judgments come to pass.

3. It is God's purpose to reveal himself. All of these things happened in order that people might know of God and believe in him. Exodus 10:2b, "that you may know that I am the Lord."

4. People need to know about God. God reveals himself to mankind in history as deliverer in the areas of real human need. His promises for the future are rooted in his acts of deliverance in the past and the present.

5. God is sovereign over the world of nature. The plagues are all

Exodus

divinely imposed natural phenomena. Exodus 9:29b, "that you may know that the earth is the Lord's."

GOALS
1. To discuss and explain the basic concepts so each pupil can relate them in his or her own words

2. To understand that God is merciful and longsuffering seeking the repentance of the sinner

3. To further appreciate that God is consistent and persistent. He will carry out his purposes.

DISCUSSION QUESTIONS
1. Do you see any significance in the sequence or order of the various plagues?

2. If you had been an Egyptian experiencing the various plagues, what would you have thought or done?

3. What do the plagues teach us about God?

PROJECTS
1. Write cinquain (five line stanza) verses using such nouns as frogs, gnats, flies, boils, hail, locusts, darkness, Moses, Aaron, and Pharoah. The students can each read independently a passage from the lesson in order to write their poetry. Following is a suggested form:
   a. choose a word
   b. write two words to describe the word
   c. write three words to say what it does or how it moves
   d. write two words that tell something special about it
   e. write the chosen noun again or synonym

   Examples: frogs (Ex. 8:1-15)   Pharoah
               jumping, hopping   stubborn, hardened
               leaving the Nile   refused Israel's freedom
               covering land   wouldn't listen
               amphibians   king

2. Illustrate the verses.

3. Let various grade levels exchange their work or post it on a bulletin board.

GREEN LEAF BIBLE SERIES

Teacher's Outline

THE BOOK OF EXODUS

LESSON #5, THE PASSOVER

PASSAGE TO STUDY: Exodus 11:1-13:16

SUGGESTIONS FOR SCRIPTURE TO BE READ IN CLASS

Basic	Supplementary
Exodus 11:1-10	Psalm 77:11-20
Exodus 12:1-13	Psalm 78:12-16, 51-55
Exodus 12:21-28	Hebrews 9:11-10:31
Exodus 12:29-42	John 1:29
Exodus 13:1-10	I Corinthians 5:7,8
	Revelation 7:14

SCRIPTURE MEMORY FOR MAY
Romans 10:9,10, "if you confess with your lips that Jesus is Lord and believe in your heart that God raised him from the dead, you will be saved. For man believes with his heart and so is justified, and he confesses with his lips and so is saved."

BASIC CONCEPTS
1. God is absolutely powerful. Nothing can stand in the way of his purposes. Egypt, the most powerful nation in the world at that time, was unable to resist God's power.

2. God is restrained in the use of his power. The potent displays of God's might, associated with the Exodus, are unusual. The final Day of Judgment is in the future: "...he has fixed a day on which he will judge the world in righteousness..." (Acts 17:31)

3. God is able to save and deliver those who call on him (in this case the people of Israel). God is the author of salvation.

4. The Passover is a sign of substitution in salvation: the lamb being sacrificed in place of the firstborn in each family just as Jesus died on the cross in place of the sinner.

5. Unleavened bread stands for the concept of purity before a Holy God. Great diligence should be involved in rooting out sin.

GOALS
1. To understand the uniqueness of the Exodus:

Exodus

    a. it is one of the major foundations of Israel's belief
    b. only a few other demonstrations of God's power are in any way comparable

2. To understand the idea of a substitute for salvation. An animal died that the first born might live. Christ died that all who believe in him may have eternal life.

DISCUSSION QUESTIONS
1. Why did God use such drastic means to secure the deliverance of the people of Israel?

2. What lessons did the people of Israel learn from that first Passover observance?

3. Why did God tell the people of Israel to keep the Passover as an annual observance?

PROJECTS
1. Have students imagine that they are one of the Israelites listening to Moses' instructions from God concerning the Passover. Prepare a check list of items which need to be done. Entitle the list "Ready! Set! Go!" There could be one list for men and one for women. Examples of items to be included:
    a. ask my neighbor for gold and silver jewelry (Exodus 11:2)
    b. get a yearling lamb without any blemish on the tenth (Exodus 12:3,5)
    c. see if I can share a lamb with my neighbor (Exodus 12:4)

2. Introduce the lesson with key words or phrases from today's scripture in order to find out what the students already know. Examples: first born in the land of Egypt, first month of the year, two doorposts, lintel, six hundred thousand, unleavened bread, hyssop, kneading bowls, four hundred and thirty years.

3. Have the students write a diary page of the happenings on the night of the first Passover.

4. Talk about the way modern Jews celebrate the Passover and compare the biblical account with the modern celebration.

GREEN LEAF BIBLE SERIES

THE BOOK OF EXODUS

LESSON #5, Supplementary Material

CELEBRATION OF PASSOVER BY MODERN JEWS
Called Pesach or The Festival of Unleavened Bread

1. Observed from 15th to 21st of Nisan (March-April), the first month of the Jewish calendar year. Orthodox Jews observe eight days; Reformed Jews observe seven.

2. Pesach means "skipping over" or "passing over"; thus, the Passover.

3. During the whole Passover week unleavened bread is eaten. Before Passover begins the housewife thoroughly cleans the house and carefully removes all leavened food (such as bread, flour, wine). Then the master of the house symbolically hunts in all the corners for any last bits. A few crumbs are left for him to discover. These are burned.

4. The first evening a special feast is held, called a Seder (which means order) because a special order is followed. During the Seder the Haggadah (from the Hebrew word l'hagid) or the story of the Exodus is read.

   A Seder plate is placed before the master of the house. The plate contains:
   a. Bitter herbs (usually horseradish) to remember the bitterness of slavery
   b. Haroseth (a mixture of chopped nuts, apples, raisins, etc.). This paste-like substance is a reminder of the mortar or the bricks made for the Egyptians.
   c. A roasted egg in remembrance of the old temple sacrifices.
   d. The shankbone of a lamb--a symbol of the Passover sacrifice. Before the fall of the temple in 70 A.D. the roasted lamb would be on the table.
   e. Parsley or radishes or celery, symbolizing hope and new growth of spring.

   The Seder table also contains:
   a. A plate of three cakes of unleavened bread
   b. Four ritual cups of wine for each person. These cups are said to correspond to the four statements of God promising deliverance in Exodus 6:6-7:
   "I will bring you out..."

Exodus

      "I will deliver you..."
      "I will redeem you..."
      "I will take you for my people..."
  c. An extra cup of wine for the prophet Elijah who is believed to come as a guest and to herald the coming of the Messiah
  d. Salt water, to symbolize either the bitter tears of bondage or the water of the Red Sea

5. As part of the ceremony the youngest person asks four questions. The answers to these questions explain the meaning of Passover.
   a. Why does this night differ from other nights? For on all other nights we eat either leavened or unleavened bread; why on this night only unleavened bread?
   b. On all other nights we eat all kinds of herbs; why on this night only bitter herbs?
   c. On all other nights we need not dip our herbs even once; why on this night must we dip them twice?
   d. On all other nights we eat either sitting up or reclining; why on this night do we all stand?

   Before the fall of the temple, when sacrifice was still practiced, one of the questions asked was why the meat was roasted and not stewed or boiled.

6. At the beginning of the Seder the statement is made:
   "This year we are here, but next year may we celebrate it in the Land of Israel."

   The Seder concludes with the words:
   "Next year in Jerusalem!"

GREEN LEAF BIBLE SERIES

Teacher's Outline

THE BOOK OF EXODUS

LESSON #6, THE DELIVERANCE OF ISRAEL

PASSAGE TO STUDY: Exodus 13:17-15:21

SUGGESTIONS FOR SCRIPTURE TO BE READ IN CLASS
<u>Basic</u>   <u>Supplementary</u>
Exodus 13:17-22   I Corinthians 10:1-14
Exodus 14:1-9   Hebrews 11:28,29
Exodus 14:19-31   Psalm 106:6-12

SCRIPTURE MEMORY FOR MAY
Romans 10:9,10, "if you confess with your lips that Jesus is Lord and believe in your heart that God raised him from the dead, you will be saved. For man believes with his heart and so is justified, and he confesses with his lips and so is saved."

BASIC CONCEPTS
1. God judges those who reject him. A person cannot be neutral regarding God; one's attitude toward God is not a matter of indifference.

2. In following God, it is normal to reach points when one does not see how it will be possible to continue in a particular direction. God will frequently bring help or guidance from unexpected sources.

3. God will deliver those who trust in him from experiences that could be devastating and spiritually defeating.
   a. Exodus 13:17
   b. I Corinthians 10:13

GOALS
1. To see that the experiences of Israel in Egypt are applicable to one's own life. That if one calls upon God, he will surely deliver (save) and that, even though the going gets rough, God will still be there and will complete his work of deliverance. Compare Philippians 1:6.

2. To understand that a person must either believe or not believe in God; that to remain uncommitted is not to believe. In the Passover only those who took the affirmative action of putting blood on the doorpost were spared.

Exodus

DISCUSSION QUESTION
1. If you had been one of the people of Israel, what would you have thought when you saw the pillar of cloud by day and the pillar of fire by night?

PROJECTS
1. Trace the Israelites' exodus from Egypt on a large map. Have an outline map for each student so that each one can fill in the locations mentioned in this lesson and in the lessons to come.

2. Announce that there is to be an award to recognize the "Man of the Year." Have the students write a paragraph describing Moses, his deeds and their reasons for nominating him.

3. Make a mural of the exodus. The students might use Egyptian picture-writing.

GREEN LEAF BIBLE SERIES

Teacher's Outline

THE BOOK OF EXODUS

LESSON #7, THE JOURNEY TO SINAI

PASSAGE TO STUDY: Exodus 15:22-18:27

SUGGESTIONS FOR SCRIPTURE TO BE READ IN CLASS

Basic	Supplementary
Exodus 15:22-27	Numbers 20:1-13
Exodus 16:1-8	Deuteronomy 6:16
Exodus 16:13-21	
Exodus 16:22-30	
Exodus 17:8-16	
Exodus 18:1-9	
Exodus 18:13-27	

SCRIPTURE MEMORY FOR MAY
Romans 10:9,10, "if you confess with your lips that Jesus is Lord and believe in your heart that God raised him from the dead, you will be saved. For man believes with his heart and so is justified, and he confesses with his lips and so is saved."

BASIC CONCEPTS
1. The principle of sabbath rest (see Exodus 16:4,5 and 16:22-30): God does not want people to work all the time. People show faith in God by ceasing other pursuits in order to rest and worship.

2. The victory over Amalek can be used to illustrate the principle of perseverance in prayer. Exodus 17:11, "Whenever Moses held up his hand, Israel prevailed; and whenever he lowered his hand, Amalek prevailed." (This occasion also illustrates the benefits of group prayer because Moses had Aaron and Hur to help him.)

3. While God chose Israel as his particular people, it has always been his purpose to include other peoples in his salvation. This is illustrated in the worship of God by Jethro, the father-in-law of Moses (Exodus 18:8-12). Note in Genesis 12:3 that God had all of the "families of the earth" in mind when he called Abraham.

4. God does all the things necessary to effect the salvation of those who trust in him. He not only delivered the people from Egypt, he provided for all of their needs in the wilderness including the need for the effective administration of justice (Exodus 18:13-27).

Exodus

5. The principle of delegation of authority and the sharing of responsibility (Exodus 18) is a basic principle of God for his people. This is also seen in Acts 6:1-7, where deacons are chosen to supplement the work of the disciples, and in I Peter 2:4-10, where all believers are called to be active representatives of God.

GOALS
1. To understand the principle of the manna: that God wants us to live in daily dependance upon him

2. To comprehend the geography of Exodus: the relationship of Egypt and Sinai and Canaan and the principal bodies of water

DISCUSSION QUESTIONS
1. Why were the people so quick to complain to Moses about the hardships of the wilderness? Why was their faith not greater?

2. What are some principles that God taught the people through the manna?

3. What lesson do we learn from the victory of the army of Israel over Amalek?

PROJECTS
1. Trace the journey from Egypt to Sinai on a map.

2. Discuss the reasonableness of the complaints of the people of Israel against Moses.

GREEN LEAF BIBLE SERIES

Teacher's Outline

THE BOOK OF EXODUS

LESSON #8, THE GIVING OF THE LAW AT SINAI

PASSAGE TO STUDY: Exodus 19:1-24:11

SUGGESTIONS FOR SCRIPTURE TO BE READ IN CLASS

<u>Basic</u>
Exodus 19:1-6
Exodus 20:1-17
Exodus 21:1-11
Exodus 21:12-25
Exodus 21:28-32
Exodus 22:21-27
Exodus 24:1-11 (compare Revelation 4:2,3,6a and 21:21b)

<u>Supplementary</u>
Leviticus 22
Deuteronomy 16
Psalm 106:13-18

SCRIPTURE MEMORY FOR MAY
Romans 10:9,10, "if you confess with your lips that Jesus is Lord and believe in your heart that God raised him from the dead, you will be saved. For man believes with his heart and so is justified, and he confesses with his lips and so is saved."

BASIC CONCEPTS
1. The holiness of God: because people are sinful they must maintain a distance between themselves and God.
   a. Exodus 19:10-15
   b. Exodus 19:21-25
   c. Exodus 20:1-11
   d. Exodus 20:18,19

2. God's covenant was established with the nation of Israel. See Exodus 19:5,6.

3. The will of God pervades all of life. Hence the commandments that the behavior of the people might be conformed to God's will. See Exodus 20:1-23:33.

4. God does not impose his covenants without regard to the response of people. They must be willingly accepted to be effective.
   a. Exodus 19:8
   b. Exodus 24:7

Exodus

GOALS
1. To further appreciate the grace of God in that he has willed to communicate his purposes to mankind.

2. To understand that God is looking for those who will be in a living relationship to him and who will represent him. See Exodus 19:5,6.

DISCUSSION QUESTIONS
1. Stated briefly--what was God's covenant with the people of Israel in the wilderness?

2. What do you believe were the main purposes for the ten commandments?

3. What were some of the laws, other than the ten commandments, that were given to the people of Israel?

4. Why were the people prevented from going up Mount Sinai? See especially Exodus 19:10-25.

PROJECTS
1. Compare the laws of Exodus chapters 21-23 with similar or related laws of contemporary nations or states.

2. Compare the laws of Exodus chapters 21-23 with similar or related laws of nations in the second and third millennium B.C.

3. Assign reports on the three festivals listed in Exodus 23:14-17.

4. Divide the class into committees. Have each committee read an assigned passage from Exodus 20:22-23:33 and report the information to the entire class. The American Bible Society translation of Exodus has good divisions and topic headings.

5. Have students write the ten commandments for shrink art. Simplify the wording. For example--You shall not worship any other gods.

6. Have the students write the ten commandments on tablet-shaped paper glued onto cardboard backing. Cut out as a puzzle for younger classes.

GREEN LEAF BIBLE SERIES

Teacher's Outline

THE BOOK OF EXODUS

LESSON #9, GOD GIVES THE ISRAELITES A SYSTEM OF WORSHIP

PASSAGE TO STUDY: Exodus 24:12-31:18

SUGGESTIONS FOR SCRIPTURE TO BE READ IN CLASS

Basic	Supplementary
Exodus 24:12-18	Hebrews 9:1-10
Exodus 25:1-9	
Exodus 25:10-22	
Exodus 26:31-37	
Exodus 29:1-14	
Exodus 29:15-25	
Exodus 30:1-10	
Exodus 31:12-18	

SCRIPTURE MEMORY FOR MAY
Romans 10: 9,10, "if you confess with your lips that Jesus is Lord and believe in your heart that God raised him from the dead, you will be saved. For man believes with his heart and so is justified, and he confesses with his lips and so is saved."

BASIC CONCEPTS
1. God is to be regularly worshiped in a manner appropriate to his holiness and greatness. Worship is to have a significant place in the lives of those who are in meaningful relationship to God. Attention and care are essential to proper worship of God.

2. The furnishings that were to be utilized in the worship of God were beautiful and of high quality. God is not honored by carelessness or by the handling of his affairs as if they are of secondary importance.
   a. Haggai 1:3-11
   b. Malachi 1:6-14
   c. Matthew 6:33

3. The principle of atonement for sin (Exodus 29:1-46): Offerings had to be made both for the sins of the priests and for the people. Since this atonement was incomplete, the sacrifices had to be offered continually. See Exodus 29:38,39 and compare with Hebrews 9:11-26.

Exodus

GOAL
1. To understand the purpose of an appointed priesthood. Selecting some men who could draw near to the presence of God in the tabernacle emphasized the holiness of God: that people were distant from him due to their sinfulness. Yet the priest was also a sign of hope that a relationship with God could be established.
    a. Job 9:32,33
    b. Hebrews 4:14-16
    c. I Timothy 2:5,6
    d. Hebrews 9:11-15

DISCUSSION QUESTIONS
1. What purpose was the tabernacle to serve?

2. What were the main sections of the tabernacle and what were their significances?

3. What were the main furnishings of the tabernacle and what were their purposes?

4. In general, what were the priests to do?

PROJECTS
1. Display pictures depicting an artist's concept or a model of the tabernacle or its furnishings or the priests' garments.

2. Display cloth material with similar colors to those described in Exodus chapters 25-28.

3. Construct a model of the tabernacle and its furnishings.

GREEN LEAF BIBLE SERIES

Teacher's Outline

THE BOOK OF EXODUS

LESSON #10, THE IDOLATRY OF THE ISRAELITES

PASSAGE TO STUDY: Exodus 32:1-35:3

SUGGESTIONS FOR SCRIPTURE TO BE READ IN CLASS
    Basic   Supplementary
    Exodus 32:1-6   Psalm 106:19-23
    Exodus 32:7-14
    Exodus 32:15-24
    Exodus 33:7-16
    Exodus 33:17-23
    Exodus 34:1-10
    Exodus 34:29-35

SCRIPTURE MEMORY FOR JUNE
    Galatians 6:7,8, "Do not be deceived; God is not mocked, for whatever a man sows, that he will also reap. For he who sows to his own flesh will from the flesh reap corruption; but he who sows to the Spirit will from the Spirit reap eternal life."

BASIC CONCEPTS
1. The seriousness of sin. Disobedience to God is not a trifle--but is an attack upon life itself, destroying a person's or a nation's relationship with God.
    a. Exodus 32:9,10
    b. Exodus 32:19,20
    c. Exodus 32:25-29
    d. Exodus 32:33-35

2. The importance of intercessory prayer. Moses contended for the people of God, and God spared their lives (Exodus 32:11-14).

3. The wonderful possibility of forgiveness, cleansing, and a new relationship with God.
    a. Exodus 32:30
    b. Exodus 34:6,7
    c. Exodus 34:9

4. The example of Moses in illustrating the possibility of a deep relationship with God.
    a. Exodus 33:8-11
    b. Exodus 33:17-23
    c. Exodus 34:29-35

Exodus

GOALS
1. To understand the need of everyone for a close relationship with God.

2. To understand the utter seriousness of disregard for God.

3. To be able to relate the main events regarding the people of Israel from the crossing of the Red Sea until Moses returned with the two tables of testimony.

DISCUSSION QUESTIONS
1. Why did Aaron cooperate with the people in organizing the making of the golden calf?

2. What do you think were the main spiritual problems of the people of Israel at this time?

3. What could the people of Israel have done to improve their relationship with God?

PROJECTS
1. Exodus 32:1-25, 33:1-3 and 34:1-10 could be read as a play:
   Act I, At the Camp
   Act II, On the Mountain
   Act III, Moses Confronts the Israelites
   Act IV, Moses Returns to Sinai
     Scene 1, Moses Returns to the Lord
     Scene 2, On the Mountain
   One method for easy reading would be to underline each part in a separate copy of Exodus in Today's English Version.

2. Have the students illustrate the events in Exodus 33:1-23. Divide a sheet of paper into six squares. Use the first square for a title. Have the students draw a picture for each of the following verses: 1-4; 5,6; 7; 8-11; and 12-23 in the remaining squares. Write a sentence summary for each picture.

3. Write the events listed in Goal 3 out of sequential order. Have the students arrange the events in the proper order.

4. Suppose that Moses assigned artists to draw posters to be displayed around camp to remind the Israelites of specific laws of God's covenant. Assign posters for students to design from Exodus 34:17-28; 35:1-3).

GREEN LEAF BIBLE SERIES

Teacher's Outline

THE BOOK OF EXODUS

LESSON #11, THE CONSTRUCTION AND FURNISHING OF THE TABERNACLE

PASSAGE TO STUDY: Exodus 35:4-40:38

SUGGESTIONS FOR SCRIPTURE TO BE READ IN CLASS

Basic	Supplementary
Exodus 35:4-9	Acts 7:44
Exodus 35:20-29	Revelation 15:5-16:1
Exodus 36:2-7	Revelation 21:1-4
Exodus 38:21-31	Hebrews 8:1-13
Exodus 40:1-15	Hebrews 9:1-14
Exodus 40:16-33	Hebrews 9:23-28
Exodus 40:34-38	Hebrews 10:19-25
	Luke 23:44-46

SCRIPTURE MEMORY FOR JUNE
Galatians 6:7,8, "Do not be deceived; God is not mocked, for whatever a man sows, that he will also reap. For he who sows to his own flesh will from the flesh reap corruption; but he who sows to the Spirit will from the Spirit reap eternal life."

BASIC CONCEPTS
1. The generous response of the offering (Exodus 36:3-7): When people catch a vision of what God wants to accomplish, an abundance of resources will become available.

2. The concept of holiness (see also Lesson #8, Basic Concept 1): The Holy of Holies was the dwelling place of God. No man was to enter it except for the high priest once a year, when properly consecrated and bringing an offering.

3. The priesthood was established so that people might have a continuing relationship with a holy God.

4. The tabernacle provided a way for people to draw close to God. It signified fellowship between God and people. Although God is holy, he provides a means whereby people may have fellowship with him. It symbolized that God provides a way of forgiveness for those who have broken his law.

Exodus

GOALS
1. To be able to identify the major sections of the tabernacle and its furnishings

2. To be able to name and identify the main people in the book of Exodus

3. To be able to explain the connection between Jesus Christ and the tabernacle

DISCUSSION QUESTIONS
1. Why were the people so generous in the offering they brought? See Exodus 36:2-7.

2. Why are we given such a complete description of the materials, furnishings, and construction of the tabernacle?

3. Can we derive some principles from this passage for our work in the local church?

PROJECTS
1. Have each student make his or her own outline drawing of the tabernacle and its furnishings.

2. Have each student tell the basic facts about one of the people in the book of Exodus other than Moses.

3. Have the students discuss the skills and abilities which God has given them. Discuss a proper stewardship of these abilities (Exodus 35:30-36:2).

4. Have the students design winged animals (Exodus 36:35). These could be transferred onto cloth and embroidered. This project could be completed during the review lesson.

GREEN LEAF BIBLE SERIES

Teacher's Outline

THE BOOK OF EXODUS

Review Questions

1. How many sons did Jacob have? _____

2. About how long were the people of Israel in Egypt from the time of Joseph until the Exodus? _____

3. What measure did the Egyptians adopt in an attempt to control the population increase of the Hebrews? _____
_____

4. What was the name of Moses' sister? _____

5. What was the name of Moses' brother? _____

6. List the three major periods in Moses' life:

    a. _____

    b. _____

    c. _____

7. What three signs did God give to Moses?

    a. _____

    b. _____

    c. _____

8. How many of the nine plagues can you list?

    a. _____   f. _____

    b. _____   g. _____

    c. _____   h. _____

    d. _____   i. _____

    e. _____

Exodus

9. Can you list four things that the people of Israel were to do in connection with the last plague and their deliverance?

   a. _____

   b. _____

   c. _____

   d. _____

10. How did the people of Israel know what route to take as they entered the wilderness? _____
_____

11. What was the problem at Marah? _____

12. What did God tell Moses to do in order to solve that problem? _____
_____

13. What provisions did God make so that the people might have food in the wilderness? _____

14. With what people or tribe did the Israelites engage in battle in the wilderness? _____

    Who was the military leader of the Israelites? _____

15. What was the name of Moses' father-in-law? _____

16. What advice did he give to Moses? _____
_____

17. Can you briefly state the ten commandments?

    a. _____

    b. _____

    c. _____

    d. _____

GREEN LEAF BIBLE SERIES

    e. _____

    f. _____

    g. _____

    h. _____

    i. _____

    j. _____

18. What was the connection or relationship between the ten commandments and the tabernacle? _____
_____

19. How were the materials provided for the tabernacle? _____
_____

20. What were the three main sections of the tabernacle and the furnishings of each section?

    a. _____

        1) _____

    b. _____

        1) _____

        2) _____

        3) _____

    c. _____

        1) _____

        2) _____

21. What great act of rebellion took place while Moses was on Mt. Sinai?
_____

Exodus

22. What were some of the consequences of that rebellion? _____
_____
_____

23. What do we learn about God from this rebellion? _____
_____
_____
_____

24. Who is the hero of the book of Exodus? _____
Why? _____
_____

HEROES OF THE BIBLE

Unit Four   The Apostle Paul
Part One   11 Weeks

GREEN LEAF BIBLE SERIES

YEAR ONE, UNIT FOUR

THE LIFE OF PAUL, PART I

Week One	INTRODUCTION TO PAUL BACKGROUND AND CONVERSION	Acts 7:54-8:3 Acts 9:1-25
Week Two	PAUL'S PREPARATION AND EARLY MINISTRY	Acts 9:26-32 Acts 11:19-30 Acts 12:25
Week Three	FIRST MISSIONARY JOURNEY	Acts 13:1-14:28
Week Four	THE COUNCIL AT JERUSALEM	Acts 15:1-35
Week Five	INTRODUCTION TO GALATIANS WARNING AGAINST FALSE GOSPELS	Galatians 1:1-2:21
Week Six	GALATIANS: JUSTIFICATION	Galatians 3:1-4:31
Week Seven	GALATIANS: CHRISTIAN LIBERTY	Galatians 5:1-6:18
Week Eight	INTRODUCTION TO COLOSSIANS CHRISTIAN DOCTRINE	Colossians 1:1-2:23
Week Nine	COLOSSIANS: CHRISTIAN LIFE	Colossians 3:1-4:18
Week Ten	PHILEMON	Philemon 1-25
Week Eleven	REVIEW AND QUIZ	

THE LIFE OF PAUL, PART I

CURRICULUM RESOURCE LIST   APPROXIMATE PRICE

BOOKS

Paul, Apostle for Today, G. A. Turner; Tyndale House (available from Cokesbury)	7.95
Pocket Size Portions; American Bible Society	.15
Acts: King James Version, Today's English Version, Revised Standard Version	
Galatians, Thessalonians: King James Version, Today's English Version	
Standard Bible Commentaries: Acts; Standard	7.95
The Acts: Then and Now; Scripture Press	2.95
Commentaries on the New Testament:	
The Epistle of Paul to the Galatians	4.95
The Epistles of Paul to the Colossians and to Philemon	4.95
Paul, Apostle of the Heart Set Free, F.F. Bruce; Eerdmans	13.95
Paul, An Outline of His Theology, Herman Ridderbos; Eerdmans	12.95
Bible Story Cartoons, Norman Lynch; Standard Book 24: "The Early Church"	.89

Arch Books; Concordia
   "The Man Who Changed His Name"
   "Paul and the Unfriendly Town"
	.79

Bible Adventures (Luke 2 and 15); Standard	4.95
If You Lived in Bible Times, Nancy Williamson; Fictor	6.95
Bible Heroes Series: Paul; Standard	1.95

MAPS, CHARTS, TIMELINES

Journeys of Paul Map Project; Scripture Press	1.65
Acts Map and Chart; Standard	2.50

TRANSPARENCIES, DUPLICATING MASTERS, FILMSTRIPS, FILMS

The Story of Paul; American Bible Society Film Purchase	40.00
Rental	7.50
God's Church in Action (overhead transparencies and ditto masters); Scripture Press	7.95

FLANNELGRAPH, POSTERS, PICTURES

Pictograph: Early Life of Paul; Standard	4.50
Annie Vallotton Posters; American Bible Society (line drawings from the Good News Bible, set of 12)	4.00

GREEN LEAF BIBLE SERIES

ACTIVITY BOOKS, PROJECTS, GAMES, PUZZLES

Bible Times Activity Books: First Christians; David C. Cook	1.99
Workbook on the Book of Acts; Standard	1.50
Bible Heroes Game; David C. Cook	3.50
Life and Letters of Paul; Find a Word Puzzle; Standard	1.50
Double Trouble Puzzles; Standard	1.50

    Acts of the Apostles
    Paul's Letters to the Churches
    Bible People from the Book of Acts

ONGOING PROJECTS

1. On a map of the Palestine and Mediterranean areas locate and mark the places where significant events concerning Paul took place.

2. Begin a wall chart about Paul, listing important facts about him as they are studied. When each letter is studied, summarize in one sentence what the book is about. Illustrate the chart.

Paul, I

Teacher's Outline

THE LIFE OF PAUL, PART I

LESSON #1, INTRODUCTION TO PAUL, BACKGROUND AND CONVERSION

PASSAGE TO STUDY: Acts 7:54-8:3 and 9:1-25

SUGGESTIONS FOR SCRIPTURE TO BE READ IN CLASS

Basic	Supplementary
Acts 7:54-8:3	Galatians 1:11-24
Acts 9:1-9	Acts 22:3-29
Acts 9:10-19a	Acts 26:9-20
Acts 19:19b-31	I Corinthians 15:7-11
	II Corinthians 22:21b-33
	Philippians 3:5,6

SCRIPTURE MEMORY FOR JUNE
   Galatians 6:7,8, "Do not be deceived; God is not mocked, for whatever a man sows, that he will also reap. For he who sows to his own flesh will from the flesh reap corruption; but he who sows to the Spirit will from the Spirit reap eternal life."

BASIC CONCEPTS
  1. Persecution against the church began immediately, and it has taken many forms over the centuries.
     a. Matthew 5:11,12, "Blessed are you when men revile you and persecute you and utter all kinds of evil against you falsely on my account. Rejoice and be glad, for your reward is great in heaven, for so men persecuted the prophets who were before you."
     b. Luke 21:12,13, "But before all this they will lay their hands on you and persecute you, delivering you up to the synagogues and prisons, and you will be brought before kings and governors for my name's sake. This will be a time for you to bear testimony."
     c. John 15:20, "Remember the word that I said to you, 'A servant is not greater than his master.' If they persecuted me, they will persecute you;..."

  2. The persecution under Saul of Tarsus led to the further growth of the church.
     a. Acts 8:4
     b. Acts 11:19
     c. Nonetheless, the scriptures recognize it as a blessing when that persecution ceased (Acts 9:31).

GREEN LEAF BIBLE SERIES

3. The conversion of Paul (Saul of Tarsus) resulted from the direct intervention of God in his life. It was not the unaided outcome of his own thought or consideration regarding Jesus Christ.
   a. Acts 9:3-9
   b. Acts 22:6-10
   c. Galatians 1:11,12, "For I would have you know, brethren, that the gospel which was preached by me is not man's gospel. For I did not receive it from man, nor was I taught it, but it came through a revelation of Jesus Christ."

4. The dramatic change in Paul is one of the great evidences of the reality of Jesus Christ (compare I Corinthians 15:7-11). It was very much a part of the case for Christianity which he presented before King Agrippa (Acts 26:2-23).

GOALS
1. To understand and be able to state in one's own words the basic facts relating to Paul before, during, and immediately following his conversion

2. To be able to locate the following places on a map:
   a. Judea   f. Cilicia
   b. Samaria   g. Jerusalem
   c. Galilee   h. Tarsus
   d. Syria   i. Damascus
   e. Phoenicia   j. Caesarea

3. To understand that while persecution is not to be invited or desired by the Christian neither is it to be considered abnormal. I Peter 4:12, "Beloved, do not be surprised at the fiery ordeal which comes upon you to prove you, as though something strange were happening to you."

4. To understand that belief in Jesus Christ is super-rational. It is not contrary to reason, but it goes beyond reason.

DISCUSSION QUESTIONS
1. Ask some of the students to share how they came to believe in Jesus Christ. At some point the teacher might share his or her own experience. Make it plain that there is not an approved way, and that all who believe do not necessarily have the type of experience that Paul did.

2. Discuss whether or not Christians in our own city or county experience persecution, and if so what forms it might take.

3. Why was Saul (Paul) so strongly opposed to Christianity?

Paul, I

4. Why do you suppose God allowed Saul to lose his sight for three days? Does this tell us anything about experiences that we ourselves might go through?

PROJECTS
1. Prepare a map depicting the spread of Christianity up to the time of Paul's conversion.

2. Prepare a poster on Damascus with a map, pictures, and Bible references.

GREEN LEAF BIBLE SERIES

Teacher's Outline

THE LIFE OF PAUL, PART I

LESSON #2, PAUL'S PREPARATION AND EARLY MINISTRY

PASSAGE TO STUDY: Acts 9:26-31; 11:19-30; 12:25-13:3

SUGGESTIONS FOR SCRIPTURE TO BE READ IN CLASS

Basic	Supplementary
Acts 9:26-31	Romans 7:4-8:4
Acts 11:19-30	II Corinthians 11:22-33
Acts 12:25-13:3	Galatians 1:11-2:5
	Philippians 3:3-11

SCRIPTURE MEMORY FOR JUNE
Galatians 6:7,8, "Do not be deceived; God is not mocked, for whatever a man sows, that he will also reap. For he who sows to his own flesh will from the flesh reap corruption; but he who sows to the Spirit will from the Spirit reap eternal life."

BASIC CONCEPTS
1. The Apostle Paul's preparation for ministry:
   a. from Tarsus: a large Greek city with a renowned university. Greek was probably Paul's primary language. He was well prepared to communicate in the great cities of the Mediterranean world of his day. Populous and cosmopolitan gentile cities would not seem strange or unfamiliar to Paul.
   b. a Jew: He would be instructed in the Old Testament scriptures. He would be prepared to expect a coming messiah. He would also feel at home in the Jewish synagogue. Acts 9:22, "But Saul increased all the more in strength, and confounded the Jews who lived in Damascus by proving that Jesus was the Christ."
   c. a Pharisee and a student of Gamaliel: He thoroughly understood Judaism, and always made his initial appeal to Jews. Having attempted so fervently to keep the law, he could more readily appreciate the gospel of grace. Romans 8:1-4, "There is therefore now no condemnation for those who are in Christ Jesus. For the law of the Spirit of life in Christ Jesus has set me free from the law of sin and death. For God has done what the law, weakened by flesh, could not do: sending his own Son in the likeness of sinful flesh and for sin, he condemned sin in the flesh, in order that the just requirement of the law might be fulfilled in us, who walk not according to the flesh but according to the Spirit."

Paul, I

    d. <u>a leader and a person of great zeal</u>: Acts 9:3, "But Saul laid waste the church and entering house after house, he dragged off men and women and committed them to prison." Acts 9:1,2, "But Saul, still breathing threats and murder against the disciples of the Lord, went to the high priest and asked him for letters to the synagogues at Damascus, so that if he found any belonging to the Way, men or women, he might bring them bound to Jerusalem."

    e. <u>a vital and dramatic encounter with Jesus Christ</u>: Paul's life was suddenly changed. Again and again his knowledge of this pivotal point in his life inspired and encouraged him in his ministry.

2. The involvement of the Holy Spirit in effective ministry:
   a. Acts 1:8
   b. Acts 2:4
   c. Acts 7:55
   d. Acts 9:31
   e. Acts 11:28
   f. Acts 13:2

3. Barnabas played a key role in bringing Paul into effective ministry in the church.

GOALS
1. To understand that Paul began effective witness for Christ almost from the beginning of his ministry. However, he was also in a protracted period of preparation that would fit him for the great missionary journeys and beyond.

2. To begin to formulate an outline of the life of the Apostle Paul

3. To appreciate the value of Barnabas' ministry

DISCUSSION QUESTIONS
1. Why was it so difficult for some Christians to accept the genuineness of Paul's conversion?

2. What are some valuable lessons to be learned from the church at Antioch?

PROJECTS
1. Prepare a report or study on Barnabas.

2. Do a background study of Antioch in the first century A.D. Illustrate with pictures.

GREEN LEAF BIBLE SERIES

Teacher's Outline

THE LIFE OF PAUL, PART I

LESSON #3, THE FIRST MISSIONARY JOURNEY

PASSAGE TO STUDY: Acts 13:1-14:28

SUGGESTIONS FOR SCRIPTURE TO BE READ IN CLASS

Basic	Supplementary
Acts 13:1-13:3	Galatians 1:1-12
Acts 13:4-12	II Corinthians 11:24-33
Acts 13:13-25	
Acts 13:42-52	
Acts 14:1-7	

SCRIPTURE MEMORY FOR JULY
Colossians 3:1,2, "If then you have been raised with Christ, seek the things that are above, where Christ is, seated at the right hand of God. Set your minds on things that are above, not on things that are on earth."

BASIC CONCEPTS
1. The cooperative nature of the First Missionary Journey: It was instituted by the Holy Spirit through the church in Antioch (Acts 13:1-3). It involved Paul, Barnabas and for the first portion, John Mark, also.

2. There was considerable receptivity to the gospel along with substantial opposition.
    a. Acts 13:6-12
    b. Acts 13:42-50
    c. Acts 14:1-7
    d. Acts 14:19-22

3. The methodology of Paul and Barnabas included preaching to the Jews first and then to the Gentiles.
    a. Acts 13:5
    b. Acts 13:13-16
    c. Acts 13:46-48
    d. Acts 14:1

4. Paul and Barnabas always worked in the largest cities in the areas that they went to with the obvious intent that the church would spread from the urban centers to the outlying districts. Acts 13:49, "And the word of the Lord spread throughout all the region."

Paul, I

GOALS
1. To be able to locate on a map all of the places visited by Paul and Barnabas on the First Missionary Journey

2. To be able to recount the main events in Paul's life from his birth in Tarsus until the beginning of his ministry in Antioch

DISCUSSION QUESTIONS
1. What important factors or events led up to the First Missionary Journey?

2. What were some of the key things that Paul emphasized when he spoke in the synagogues?

3. How would you characterize the response to Paul and Barnabas as they proclaimed the gospel in the cities of Galatia?

4. How did Paul and Barnabas respond to severe opposition? What would you have done in similar circumstances?

PROJECTS
1. Have each student trace the First Missionary Journey on an outline map.

2. Have someone give a brief report on John Mark.

3. Have someone do a background report with illustrations on Antioch of Syria (Acts 13:1).

GREEN LEAF BIBLE SERIES

Teacher's Outline

THE LIFE OF PAUL, PART I

LESSON #4, THE COUNCIL AT JERUSALEM

PASSAGE TO STUDY: Acts 15:1-35

SUGGESTIONS FOR SCRIPTURE TO BE READ IN CLASS
<table>
<tr><td>Basic</td><td>Supplementary</td></tr>
<tr><td>Acts 15:1-5</td><td>Galatians 1:6-10</td></tr>
<tr><td>Acts 16:6-11</td><td>Galatians 5:1-12</td></tr>
<tr><td>Acts 15:12-21</td><td>Romans 4:1-12</td></tr>
<tr><td>Acts 15:22-29</td><td></td></tr>
<tr><td>Acts 15:30-35</td><td></td></tr>
</table>

SCRIPTURE MEMORY FOR JULY
Colossians 3:1,2, "If then you have been raised with Christ, seek the things that are above, where Christ is, seated at the right hand of God. Set your minds on things that are above, not on things that are on earth."

BASIC CONCEPTS
1. The Judaizers, who proclaimed the necessity of circumcision, raised such a serious issue that Paul and Barnabas went on a considerable journey and the church had a very significant meeting to deal with it.

2. There are some matters of such import that time must be taken out of one's usual responsibilities to deal with them.

3. James, the brother of Jesus, was the evident leader of the church in Jerusalem.
    a. Acts 15:13
    b. Acts 21:18
    c. Galatians 1:19
    d. Galatians 2:9,12

4. The gospel of salvation by grace could not include requiring gentiles to become proselytes to Judaism before they became Christians.

5. The decision of the Jerusalem Council was monumental in freeing the gentile church from becoming Jewish proselytes as a part of believing in Jesus Christ and, thus, assuring that the gospel was clearly one of grace unhindered by trappings of works. The book

Exodus

of Galatians spells out in detail the effects of the Jerusalem Council.

DISCUSSION QUESTIONS
1. Why was the issue of circumcision dealt with in Jerusalem? Why not in some other locale?

2. What reasons or arguments carried the day so that it was agreed that gentile converts need not be circumcised?

3. What do we learn about the nature of the relationships or organization of the early church from this passage?

PROJECTS
1. Develop a map showing the extent of the church at the time of the Jerusalem Council.

2. Select two groups to represent in discussion (rather than simulate) the various points of view in the Jerusalem Council.

GREEN LEAF BIBLE SERIES

GALATIANS

Author: Paul, Apostle of Jesus Christ

Date of Writing: 53-55 A.D.

Place of Writing: Probably Corinth or Ephesus

Destination: The churches in the Roman Province of Galatia: Lystra, Iconium, Derbe, Antioch of Pisidia

Purpose: Paul is obviously greatly distressed that the pure and simple gospel of faith and grace that he had proclaimed in Galatia is being corrupted. He affirms the superiority of this gospel to false ones that add legalistic concepts that will reenslave people.

Background: Galatians is one of the most theological writings in the whole Bible. With the possible exception of Romans, nowhere is the gospel of grace set forth with more system and clarity. Recognizing that for the past nineteen hundred years the church has fallen into many of the errors that Paul mentions--one wonders if the gospel would have survived without the corrective influence of the book of Galatians.

North Galatia vs. South Galatia: The cities mentioned in Acts 13:14-14:23 where Paul and Barnabas established churches on the First Missionary Journey are in what is known as South Galatia. Galatia derives its name from the immigration into Asia of a large body of Gauls from Europe about 278 B.C. The Roman province was expanded to include areas south of where these Gauls lived. The churches mentioned in Acts are Pisidian Antioch, Iconium, Lystra, and Derbe. These cities were in the southern part of the Roman province of Galatia and were some distance south of "Old Galatia" where the Gauls had settled. The question is whether Paul's letter to the Galatians was addressed to these four churches mentioned in Acts or if the letter was addressed to some unknown churches of "Old Galatia." Since it is not specifically mentioned that Paul founded churches in North Galatia, the presumption is that these four cities mentioned in Acts are the ones to whom the letter was addressed.

Galatians was probably written after the Council at Jerusalem (approximately 49 A.D.). Some contend that since Paul does not refer to the Council at Jerusalem (Acts 15:6-29) in this letter that Galatians must have been written prior to that council. This argument from silence is inconclusive. Paul is concerned that the gospel that he proclaims stand on its own feet. He received it directly from Jesus Christ (1:11,12). Indeed, a reference to the Council of Jerusalem in this context might undermine Paul's point that the gospel which he preached was received by direct revelation from God. The idea put forth by some, that this letter was written from Antioch shortly after the First Missionary Journey, seems not to allow sufficient time for the growth of the church so that false preachers would be attracted to it.

It seems likely that Paul does refer to the Council at Jerusalem in Galatians 2:1-10. The major problem is Paul's reference to presenting his gospel privately (Galatians 2:2). However, this may only mean that he did not preach in Jerusalem, but that he confined his remarks to private conversations and to the relative privacy of the Council. Those who contend for an earlier date for Galatians assume that Paul must mention the Jerusalem Council if it has taken place. If this is the case, why does he not mention it in his other letters, which almost all concede were written after that Council? And how is it that the Judaizers reached considerably more distant Galatia before they reached Antioch (Acts 15:1)? One of the best discussions of this issue is found in Introduction to the New Testament by Everett F. Harrison (Eerdmans Publishing Co.).

OUTLINE
- A. Introduction (1:1-2:14)
  1. Greeting (1:1-5)
  2. Warning against perverting the gospel (1:6-9)
  3. Paul defends his gospel (1:10-2:14)
     a. he received it directly from Jesus Christ (1:10-17)
     b. Paul's equality with the apostles (1:18-2:14)
        1) first visit with Peter (1:18-20)
        2) Paul preaches in Syria (1:21-24)
        3) second visit to Jerusalem (2:1-8)
        4) Paul and Barnabas are accepted (2:9,10)
        5) Peter at Antioch (2:11-14)

- B. Justification by Faith (2:15-5:12)
  1. Right standing with God comes through faith not law (2:15-21)
  2. The Spirit came by faith not works (3:1-5)
  3. Abraham was made righteous through faith (3:6-9)
  4. The righteous live by faith (3:10-14)
  5. Some explanations regarding the law (3:15-25)
     a. it did not annul the promise which had already been made to Abraham (3:15-18)
     b. it was given because of man's sinfulness (3:19-20)
     c. it does not contradict God's promise (3:21,22)
     d. it was given to restrain sin (3:23-25)

GREEN LEAF BIBLE SERIES

        6. The benefits of sonship have been conferred through faith (3:26-4:7)
           a. all who believe in Jesus Christ are sons of God through faith (3:26-29)
           b. those who believe in Christ are no longer under the Old Covenant (4:1-5)
           c. the presence of the Holy Spirit in a believer's life is an evidence of his sonship (4:6,7)

        7. The observance of the festivals under the Old Covenant [by gentiles] indicates a departure from faith (4:8-10)

        8. Paul appeals to his love for them and their previous loyalty to him (4:12-20)

        9. Freedom under the New Covenant is contrasted with slavery under the Old Covenant (4:21-5:12)
           a. the allegory of Sarah and Hagar (4:21-5:1)
           b. the danger of advocating circumcision (5:2-12)

C. New Laws for the Christian (5:13-6:10)
    1. Love your neighbor (5:13-15)

    2. Be guided by the Spirit (5:16-25)

    3. What to do when somebody sins (6:1-5)
       a. help him in gentleness (6:1)
       b. don't become proud (6:2-5)

    4. Share with those who minister to you (6:6-10)
       a. don't think you can deceive God (6:7,8)
       b. remember God will reward (6:9,10)

D. Paul's Personal Conclusion (6:11-18)
    1. He emphasizes the cross and a new creation (6:11-16)

    2. He has suffered for Christ's sake (6:17)

    3. Benediction (6:18)

Paul, I

Teacher's Outline

THE LIFE OF PAUL, PART I

LESSON #5, INTRODUCTION TO GALATIANS/WARNING AGAINST FALSE
    GOSPELS

PASSAGE TO STUDY: Galatians 1:1-2:21

SUGGESTIONS FOR SCRIPTURE TO BE READ IN CLASS
    Basic
    Galatians 1:1-9
    Galatians 1:10-24
    Galatians 2:1-10
    Galatians 2:11-14
    Galatians 2:15-21

SCRIPTURE MEMORY FOR JULY
    Colossians 3:1,2, "If then you have been raised with Christ, seek the things that are above, where Christ is, seated at the right hand of God. Set your minds on things that are above, not on things that are on earth."

BASIC CONCEPTS
1. The authentic gospel has come from Jesus Christ, and has been given to the Apostle Paul by direct revelation. Any other "gospels" which contradict the gospel that Paul has given to them are to be rejected.

2. The authenticity of Paul's gospel is supported by the full acceptance of his ministry by the leaders of the church in Jerusalem.

3. People are not justified by works of the law, but through faith in Jesus Christ (Galatians 2:16).

4. The good that the Christian does is the effect of his salvation, not the cause of it. His "good works" are the product of Jesus Christ who lives within him.

GOALS
1. To help each person to understand the doctrinal conflicts in the church that prompted the writing of the book of Galatians

2. To review the pertinent historical materials relating to Peter, Paul, and the first missionary journey so that each person might

GREEN LEAF BIBLE SERIES

    have a good foundation for understanding Galatians

DISCUSSION QUESTIONS
1. What has happened in the churches of Galatia that disturbs Paul?

2. Where is the <u>authority</u> for the gospel?

3. Why does Paul talk about the incident with Peter in Antioch?

PROJECTS
1. Make a list of the times that Paul was in Jerusalem.

2. Trace the movements of Paul on a map from the time of his conversion through the Second Missionary Journey.

Paul, I

Teacher's Outline

THE LIFE OF PAUL, PART I

LESSON #6, GALATIANS/JUSTIFICATION

PASSAGE TO STUDY: Galatians 3:1-4:31

SUGGESTIONS FOR SCRIPTURE TO BE READ IN CLASS

Basic	Supplementary
Galatians 3:1-9	Romans 3:21-31
Galatians 3:10-18	Romans 5:1-5
Galatians 3:19-29	
Galatians 4:1-11	
Galatians 4:12-20	
Galatians 4:21-31	

SCRIPTURE MEMORY FOR JULY
Colossians 3:1,2, "If then you have been raised with Christ, seek the things that are above, where Christ is, seated at the right hand of God. Set your minds on things that are above, not on things that are on earth."

BASIC CONCEPTS
1. In order to have a good relationship with God one must be just. Because God is just and holy he will not overlook unrighteousness.
   a. Romans 3:9-20
   b. Romans 3:23
   c. I Peter 1:15,16
   d. Matthew 5:48

2. A person cannot establish his own righteousness before God. He cannot justify himself.
   a. Galatians 2:16
   b. Galatians 2:21
   c. Galatians 3:11

3. The sinner finds his justification through faith in Jesus Christ.
   a. Galatians 2:16
   b. Galatians 3:13,14

4. To attempt to establish a relationship with God by some means other than faith in Christ is to deny Jesus Christ.
   a. Galatians 3:6-9
   b. Galatians 5:2-4

GREEN LEAF BIBLE SERIES

    5. By faith in Christ we find freedom to be led by the Holy Spirit.
       a. Galatians 5:1
       b. Romans 8:5-11
       c. Ephesians 5:18-20

GOALS
1. To understand the Galatian error: that it is utter folly to attempt to merit God's favor by one's own works

2. To understand that one is just and righteous in God's sight when he believes in Jesus Christ

DISCUSSION QUESTIONS
1. Why are all who rely on works of the law under a curse (Galatians 3:10)?

2. What purposes does the law serve?

3. What is the meaning of the analogy between Hagar and Sarah?

PROJECTS
1. Have the students write out Galatians 2:15-21 in their own words.

2. Divide a sheet of notebook paper into two columns. Head one column, "The benefits of faith"; head the other column, "The Law." List words or phrases under each column with the verse reference from Galatians 2:15-5:12.

Paul, I

Teacher's Outline

THE LIFE OF PUAL, PART I

LESSON #7, GALATIANS/CHRISTIAN LIBERTY

PASSAGE TO STUDY: Galatians 5:1-6:18

SUGGESTIONS FOR SCRIPTURE TO BE READ IN CLASS
Basic
Galatians 5:1-12
Galatians 5:13-25
Galatians 6:1-10
Galatians 6:11-18

SCRIPTURE MEMORY FOR AUGUST
Colossians 3:17, "And whatever you do, in word or deed, do everything in the name of the Lord Jesus, giving thanks to God the Father through him."

BASIC CONCEPTS
1. Those who would be justified by the law are severed from Christ. They have fallen away from grace.

2. The Christian is set free from the requirements of the law, but he should be careful lest he use his freedom as an opportunity for the flesh.

3. Although he is set free from the law, the Christian is given new guidelines:
   a. he is to love his neighbor
   b. he is to be guided by the Holy Spirit
   c. he is to gently help those who sin
   d. he is to do good unto all people

4. Those who advocated a false gospel were improperly motivated in that they sought to avoid persecution for the cross of Christ.

GOALS
1. To understand the consequences of spiritual or fleshly choices on our lives. That is, our choices will result in the fruits of the spirit (3:22-23) or the works of the flesh (3:19-21).

2. To realize that morality is absolute, not relative or culturally determined.

GREEN LEAF BIBLE SERIES

    3. To understand that many moral principles that are commonly taken for granted derive from the Bible

DISCUSSION QUESTIONS
1. In what sense has the Christian been set free in Christ?

2. When Paul speaks of "the law" in the book of Galatians, what specifically is he talking about?

3. What is the main point of Galatians 6:6-10?

PROJECT
Find parallels of "works of the flesh" and "fruits of the spirit" in the writings of Moses (Genesis, Exodus, Leviticus, Numbers, Deuteronomy) and those about Jesus (Matthew, Mark, Luke, John) to show the continuity of God's moral teaching.

Paul, I

COLOSSIANS

Author: Paul, Apostle of Jesus Christ

Date of Writing: Approximately 61 A.D.

Destination: The church at Colossae, in the Roman province of Asia

Purpose: To urge them to continue their growth in Jesus Christ, and not to be led astray by false philosophical teachings

Background: The book of Acts gives us no certain evidence of a visit by Paul to the city of Colossae. However, Paul and his associates probably passed through Colossae on the third missionary journey. Acts 18:23 states that Paul went through the region of Galatia and Phrygia, and Acts 19:1, "While Apollos was at Corinth, Paul passed through the upper country and came to Ephesus." The most probable route would have taken him through the Lycus Valley and the cities of Colossae, Hierapolis, and Laodicea.

Many scholars infer from Colossians 1:4 and 2:1 that Paul did not found the church, but that it was founded by Epaphras (Colossians 1:7, 4:12,13). Colossians is one of the four "captivity epistles": Ephesians, Philippians, Colossians, and Philemon. Almost all recognize a very close relationship between Colossians and Philemon--that they were written about the same time and carried by the same messenger. Philemon appears to live in the same area as Colossae. Paul implies that he has visited in Philemon's home (Philemon 4-7) and that he has led Philemon to Christ (Philemon 19b). Therefore, if Paul had a personal ministry to Philemon and his household, there is no reason to rule out a personal ministry at Colossae.

OUTLINE OF COLOSSIANS
    A. SALUTATION (1:1,2)

        B. PRELIMINARY REMARKS (1:3-14)
          1. Paul gives thanks for their faith and love (1:3-5a)

          2. He reflects on their hearing of and growth in the gospel (1:5b-8)

          3. He prays that they may be filled with the knowledge of God's will in order that they might lead a life fully pleasing to the Lord (1:9,10)

          4. It is his desire that they might be strengthened by the power of God for endurance and patience (1:11,12)

GREEN LEAF BIBLE SERIES

        5. God has delivered us from darkness and transferred us to the kingdom of his Son (1:13,14)

  B. THE PREEMINENCE AND GLORY OF JESUS CHRIST (1:15-23)
     1. He is the image of the invisible God (1:15-17)

     2. He is preeminent in all things (1:18-20)
        a. he is the head of the church (1:18)
        b. all the fullness of God dwells in him (1:19)
        c. he is the means of reconciliation (1:20)

     3. Christ has reconciled them by his death in order to present them holy and blameless and irreproachable before God (1:21-23)

  C. PAUL LABORS FOR THE SAKE OF THE CHURCH TO PRESENT EVERY PERSON MATURE IN CHRIST (1:24-29)
     1. His sufferings contribute to the welfare of the church (1:24,25a)

     2. The word of God makes known the mystery of God's work in Jesus Christ (1:25b-27)

     3. Paul desires to so proclaim the gospel that every person may be presented mature in Jesus Christ (1:28,29)

  D. PAUL'S INSTRUCTIONS TO THE CHURCH (2:1-4:6)
     1. They are to be established in the faith (2:1-7)
        a. he puts forth great effort that many in the church may be knit together in love and that they may have the understanding and the knowledge of God's mystery in Christ (2:1-3)
        b. he does not want them to be deluded by appealing, but false talk (2:4,5)
        c. he urges them to be rooted and built up in Jesus Christ (2:6,7)

     2. He warns them against being led astray by false philosophies and practices (2:8-23)
        a. general statement (2:8)
        b. the whole fullness of deity dwells bodily in Jesus Christ (2:9)
        c. Jesus Christ has done a great work in them (2:10-15)
        d. they are not to let others pass judgment on them in regard to food or drink or festival (2:16,17)

Paul, I

       e. beware of those who insist on self-abasement and worship of angels (2:18,19)
       f. they are to avoid false human regulations (2:20-23)

    3. Seek the things that are above (3:1-17)
       a. set your minds on things that are above (3:1-4)
       b. put to death what is earthly (3:5-11)
          1) earthly defined: immorality, impurity, passion, evil desire, covetousness
          2) the wrath of God
          3) further defined: anger, wrath, malice, slander, foul talk
          4) do not lie to one another
          5) faith in Christ cuts across all human distinctions (3:11)
       c. put on godly qualities (3:12-17)
          1) basic desirable qualities defined
          2) love especially emphasized
          3) let the peace of Christ rule in your hearts
          4) be thankful
          5) let the word of Christ dwell in you richly, teaching and admonishing one another
          6) whatever you do--do in the name of the Lord Jesus

    4. Proper behavior for members of families and masters and slaves (3:18-4:1)

    5. Continue steadfastly in prayer (4:2-4)

    6. Conduct yourselves wisely toward outsiders (4:5,6)

E. CONCLUDING REMARKS (4:7-18)
    1. Tychicus and Onesimus are being sent to Colossae by Paul (4:7-9)

    2. Aristarchus, Mark, and Justus send their greetings (4:10,11)

    3. Epaphras sends greetings and always remembers them in his prayers (4:12,13)

    4. Greetings from Luke and Demas (4:14)

    5. Paul extends his greeting to the brethren at Laodicea and to Nympha (4:15)

GREEN LEAF BIBLE SERIES

    6. Instructions regarding the reading of the letter (4:16)

    7. Archippus encouraged to fulfill the ministry which he has received from the Lord (4:17)

    8. Paul's concluding statement written with his own hand (4:18)

Paul, I

Teacher's Outline

THE LIFE OF PAUL, PART I

LESSON #8, COLOSSIANS/CHRISTIAN DOCTRINE

PASSAGE TO STUDY: Colossians 1:1-2:23

SUGGESTIONS FOR SCRIPTURE TO BE READ IN CLASS
Basic	Supplementary
Colossians 1:1-14	John 1:1-14
Colossians 1:15-23	John 14:4-11
Colossians 1:24-29	
Colossians 2:1-7	
Colossians 2:8-15	
Colossians 2:16-23	

SCRIPTURE MEMORY FOR AUGUST
  Colossians 3:17, "And whatever you do, in word or deed, do everything in the name of the Lord Jesus, giving thanks to God the Father through him."

BASIC CONCEPTS
1. Paul rejoices that the gospel is making good progress at Colossae as it is throughout the whole world.

2. Paul's colleague, Epaphras, has had an important part in the ministry at Colossae.

3. It is Paul's desire that the Colossians grow in knowledge, wisdom, and understanding.

4. Jesus Christ is the image of the invisible God; by him all things were created; and by his power existence is made possible.

5. Paul's goal is that every person might achieve maturity in Jesus Christ.

6. Paul warns the Colossians against falling prey to philosophy and empty deceit.

GOALS
1. To be able to locate Colossae on a map and understand the possible relationship between Colossae and Paul's Third Missionary Journey.

GREEN LEAF BIBLE SERIES

    2. To help each person understand the relationship between Colossians and Philemon

    3. To be able to state in one's own words the basic themes or concepts of Colossians chapters one and two

DISCUSSION QUESTIONS
1. What can we learn about prayer from chapter 1?

2. Colossians has a very strong Christological emphasis. What is the apostle seeking to accomplish by that emphasis?

3. What were some of the problems of the church at Colossae indicated by chapters 1 and 2?

PROJECTS
1. Make a list of the things that Paul desires for the Colossians and illustrate with pictures or drawings by the students or make a list of those other characteristics or qualities that will enable or encourage the things that Paul mentions.

2. Make a list of verses and illustrate regarding what is said about Jesus Christ in chapters 1 and 2.

Paul, I

Teacher's Outline

THE LIFE OF PAUL, PART I

LESSON #9, COLOSSIANS/CHRISTIAN LIFE

PASSAGE TO STUDY: Colossians 3:1-4:18

SUGGESTIONS FOR SCRIPTURE TO BE READ IN CLASS
Basic	Supplementary
Colossians 3:1-11	Ephesians 4:17-5:20
Colossians 3:12-17	Romans 12:1-21
Colossians 3:18-4:1	
Colossians 4:2-9	
Colossians 4:10-18	

SCRIPTURE MEMORY FOR AUGUST
Colossians 3:17, "And whatever you do, in word or deed, do everything in the name of the Lord Jesus, giving thanks to God the Father through him."

BASIC CONCEPTS
1. The one who believes in Jesus Christ is to purposefully seek the things that are associated with Christ. He is to set his mind on the things that are above, where Christ is.

2. Earthly inclinations are to be put to death. They are identified as follows: immorality, impurity, passion, evil desire, covetousness, anger, wrath, malice, slander, foul talk, lies.

3. Believers are to deliberately cultivate those qualities which belong to the new nature, which are: compassion, kindness, lowliness, meekness, patience, forgiveness, love, the peace of Christ, and thankfulness.

4. Whatever a person does is to be done in the name of the Lord Jesus, giving thanks to God.

5. Prayer is important in enabling the work of Jesus Christ.
   a. Colossians 4:2
   b. Colossians 4:3,4
   c. Colossians 4:12

6. In witnessing to others we should approach them in a pleasing and appealing way (Colossians 4:5,6).

GREEN LEAF BIBLE SERIES

GOALS
1. To help us understand that belief in Jesus Christ involves a radical commitment of life to him so that we consciously adopt new values

2. To help us better comprehend those lists of qualities that are detrimental to life and those that are beneficial

DISCUSSION QUESTIONS
1. What is the rationale for right living or godly behavior?

2. What are some keys to living a godly life?

3. Of the things that should be put away what is the hardest for you to deal with?

4. Of those good qualities that should be put on--in what area would you most like to see personal growth in coming months?

PROJECTS
1. Make a list and illustrate those things that are to be put to death or that are to be put away.

2. Make a list and illustrate those things that are to be put on--that are to be encouraged in the Christian life.

Paul, I

PHILEMON

BACKGROUND
Author: Paul, Apostle of Jesus Christ

Date of Writing: Approximately 61 A.D.

Place of Writing: Rome, in prison (Acts 18:16)

Destination: To Philemon, probably a member of the church at Colossae or a nearby church (see Colossians 4:9)

Purpose: To secure safe return and favorable treatment for Onesimus, a runaway slave belonging to Philemon. Onesimus appears to have been converted to Christ by Paul. This letter is perhaps the only surviving example of many private letters that Paul must have written. "[The letter] owes nothing to the graces of rhetoric; its effect is due solely to the spirit of the writer." Saint Paul's Epistles to the Colossians and to Philemon, J.B. Lightfoot, Zondervan, p. 319.

OUTLINE OF PHILEMON
1. Salutation (1-3)

2. Paul compliments Philemon for his faith and service for Jesus Christ (4-7)

3. The apostle is returning Onesimus to Philemon (8-14)

4. He asks that Onesimus be received and that any wrongs be charged to Paul's account (15-21)

5. Paul indicates his plans to visit Philemon (22)

6. Concluding greetings and benediction (23-25)

THESIS
Paul is sending the slave, Onesimus, back to his Christian owner, Philemon. Paul urges Philemon to restore Onesimus to his household and to accept him as a Christian brother, assuring him that great benefits will be achieved.

GREEN LEAF BIBLE SERIES

THE LIFE OF PAUL, PART I

LESSON #10, PHILEMON

PASSAGE TO STUDY: Philemon 1-25

SUGGESTIONS FOR SCRIPTURE TO BE READ IN CLASS
Basic	Supplementary
Philemon 1-7	Colossians 4:1-18
Philemon 8-14	
Philemon 15-25	

MEMORY VERSE FOR AUGUST
   Colossians 3:17, "And whatever you do, in word or deed, do everything in the name of the Lord Jesus, giving thanks to God the Father through him."

BASIC CONCEPTS
   1. The gospel transforms lives. Onesimus has been changed from a worthless slave to a valuable partner.

   2. Paul did not try to eradicate slavery, but to temper the relationship between master and slave by teaching mutual love, respect, and fear of God (Colossians 4:1; Ephesians 6:5-9).

   3. Paul, though in prison, conducted a busy ministry. But he was not too busy to intercede in behalf of an unimportant slave.

GOAL
   To teach the student that God loves all people equally regardless of their station in life, and that it is the responsibility of those who are more favored by life to deal fairly with those who have less

DISCUSSION QUESTIONS
   1. Why is Paul able to make such a radical request of Philemon?

   2. How do you think Onesimus felt about all this?

PROJECT
   Do a study on the subject of slavery in the Bible. A further project would be to note how biblical principles contributed to the eventual

elimination of slavery. On the return of slaves to their master, see Deuteronomy 23:15,16. Also note: Colossians 4:1 and 4:7-9, and Ephesians 6:5-9, and I Corinthians 7:21ff.

GREEN LEAF BIBLE SERIES

Teacher's Outline

THE LIFE OF PAUL, PART I

LESSON #11, QUIZ

1. In what city was Paul born? _____

2. To what city was Paul sent for further training and education? _____

3. Under what great rabbi did Paul study? _____

4. What other name is frequently used for Paul in the book of Acts? ____

5. How did Saul of Tarsus "contribute" to the growth of the church before he was converted? _____

6. Paul was approaching what city when he was converted? _____

7. What was the name of the man who ministered to Paul after he went into the city? _____

8. Beginning with Paul's birth, list the places where we find him up until the beginning of his First Missionary Journey:

   a. _____   f. _____
   b. _____   g. _____
   c. _____   h. _____
   d. _____   i. _____
   e. _____

9. Who were Paul's two companions on his First Missionary Journey?

   a. _____   b. _____

Paul, I

10. What church was the base of operations for the various missionary journeys? _____

11. List the places visited on the First Missionary Journey:

   a. _____   e. _____

   b. _____   f. _____

   c. _____   g. _____

   d. _____

12. What event led to the Jerusalem Council (Acts 15)? _____
_____

13. What was the basic decision of the Jerusalem Council? _____
_____
_____

14. List four characteristics or experiences that contributed to Paul's success as a Christian minister:

   a. _____

   b. _____

   c. _____

   d. _____

15. List three methodologies or strategies evident in the First Missionary Journey:

   a. _____

   b. _____

   c. _____

16. What was the basic error that Paul sought to correct in the book of Galatians? _____

Paul, I

17. What is the "new law" set forth in Galatians? _____

    _____

18. List four important emphases of the book of Colossians:

    a. _____

    b. _____

    c. _____

    d. _____

19. List three statements that Colossians makes about Jesus Christ:

    a. _____

    b. _____

    c. _____

20. What was Paul's purpose in writing the Philemon letter? _____

    _____

    _____

21. What rationale does Paul use in seeking Philemon's cooperation?

    _____

    _____

THE GREEN LEAF BIBLE SERIES

    Year One   HEROES OF THE BIBLE

    Year Two   JOURNEYS, KINGS, AND TRIUMPHS

    Year Three   JOYFUL SERVANTS OF GOD

    Year Four   THE POWERFUL WORD OF GOD

    Year Five   THE GROWTH OF THE BELIEVING COMMUNITY

    Year Six   SONGS AND PROMISES

Green Leaf Press
P. O. Box 6880
Alhambra, CA 91802

☐ Please send _____ copies of GREEN LEAF BIBLE SERIES, Year One at $12.50 each.

☐ Please send _____ copies of GREEN LEAF BIBLE SERIES, Year Two at $12.50 each.

☐ Please send information on Year Three, JOYFUL SERVANTS OF GOD

Ship to:
Name _____

Address _____

City/State/Zip _____

☐ My check is enclosed or ☐ Please bill:
Name _____

Address _____

City/State/Zip _____

Charge my Visa ☐ or Mastercard ☐

Number _____ Expiration date _____

Signature _____

Send to Green Leaf Press, P.O. Box 6880, Alhambra, CA 91802   GLBS I